Boost Your **Intelligence**

Tested Techniques for **Improving Your IQ and EQ**

Harry Alder

KoganPage

London Philadelphia New Delhi

Indian Edition 2010

Kogan Page India Private Limited
4737/23 Ansari Road,
Daryaganj
New Delhi 110 002

This edition is for sale in the Indian subcontinent only. Not for export elsewhere.

ISBN: 978-81-7554-602-8

Published by Vinod Vasishtha for Kogan Page India Private Limited,
4737/23, Ansari Road, Daryaganj, New Delhi 110 002.

Printed and bound in India.

Contents

The Author

Dr Harry Alder draws on his vast experience as a businessperson in top corporate and public positions. He now trains senior executives in leading companies, specializing in the areas of creativity and innovation, advanced communication skills and personal effectiveness.

A popular conference speaker and broadcaster, with a truly international audience, Dr Alder has a Masters degree and doctorate in business administration. He is Associate Professor of a leading international business school and a certified NLP master practitioner. A prolific author, his many books appear in more than 15 foreign language editions.

Other books by Harry Alder:

Corporate Charisma (Piatkus)
How to Achieve Twice as Much in Half the Time (How To Books)
How to Live Longer (How To Books)
Masterstroke (Piatkus)
Mind-to-Mind Marketing (Kogan Page)
NLP for Managers (Piatkus)
NLP for Trainers (McGraw-Hill)
NLP in 21 Days (Piatkus)

NLP: The New Art and Science of Getting What You Want (Piatkus)
Quick Fix Your Emotional Intelligence (How To Books)
Remembering Names and Faces (How To Books)
The Right Brain Manager (Piatkus)
The Right Brain Time Manager (Piatkus)
The Ultimate 'How To' Book (Gower)
Think Like a Leader (Piatkus)
Train Your Brain (Piatkus)

Introduction

Some say we are born with it – or without it. Some say we pick it up as we go along, especially in the formative first few years of life, through our environment and the influence of parents and teachers. Amazingly, after centuries of philosophizing and decades of serious science, not only do we not understand human intelligence, but nor has it been satisfactorily defined. More accurately, it has been defined *ad nauseam*, but with little consensus among experts and laypeople alike.

So when it comes to being 'more intelligent' it depends on what you mean and what you want. Fortunately, it is easier to do something about the sorts of behaviour and characteristics usually *associated* with, or that *display*, intelligence than to either define it or measure it. However awesome, complex, mystical or indefinable human intelligence, you can *act* and *be* more intelligent.

We know remarkably little about the human mind in comparison with what we don't know about it. However, much of our knowledge has been gained in the last couple of decades, during which mind-related sciences have advanced at a spectacular pace. So there is a lot of knowledge that hasn't yet reached ordinary people who could benefit simply by using their brains in a better way. We now have information and techniques that allow every one of us to be 'more intelligent'.

We now know, for instance, that the idea of IQ (intelligence quotient) hardly does justice to the multi-faceted nature of intelligence. It measures a particular kind of intelligence in a particular culture for particular purposes. Specifically, it purports to measure 'left-brain' functions that we associate with language, logic, analysis, academic competence and intellect – what is often termed *cognition*. As we shall see, there's much more to intelligence than that.

In fact, there are many kinds of intelligence, and it reveals itself in many ways. An academic, 'brainy', high-IQ boffin, for instance, may be socially unintelligent, in DIY or sport, art and music, mental arithmetic, politics and such like. He or she may not display 'intelligence' in those contexts, however academically qualified. Even streetwise ten-year-olds can outsmart many high-IQ adults in some areas of life. They are *smart* – or intelligent – whatever their education and the IQ that largely measures it. So, clearly, there are different kinds, as well as degrees, of intelligence. We differ both in the kind of intelligence we 'possess', the degree to which we possess it, and – more importantly for most of us – the use we make of it in life.

Many psychologists still see intelligence as a more or less hereditary factor, measurable and predictable like height and eye colour. But a number of contemporary brain-mind researchers are suggesting that the only limits to our intelligence are self-made and relate to our beliefs about what is 'possible'. Israeli psychologist Dr Reuven Fuerstein, along with a number of others, maintains that at any age, and almost at any ability level, we can improve our mental functioning. In other words, we can be more intelligent. When we consider the variety of definitions of intelligence it is no surprise that there are widely differing opinions about the extent to which it can be improved.

It may not be true that anything is possible, but it's a useful (and intelligent) presupposition if you want to live up to your full potential. Call it optimism, positive thinking, or whatever. Confidence in yourself and your potential is a big factor in achievement and it's *smart* – intelligent – to take it into account.

Of the many definitions of intelligence, IQ is the one that strongly purports to be genetic and more or less immutable. It is also the most commonly used meaning of intelligence, and plays a large part in education, commerce and the institutions of the Western world. It can affect our lives in many ways. But we shall see that it has significant limitations, and in particular does not take account of the 'people' skills, or *social* intelligence, so important in work and personal life. Not surprisingly, in omitting these important skills, IQ does not correlate to 'success' in the sense that most of us use the term.

Despite the controversy over IQ as a measure of true intelligence, it can play an important role in many aspects of our lives, however we might personally value it and the things it purports to measure. So Chapter 2 will give IQ special attention, as an orthodox, widely used intelligence 'score'.

IQ, whatever human qualities it deems to identify, is a number – a score. It *quantifies* precisely the traits and attributes it sets out to measure. And a measurable improvement in intelligence – of whatever kind – can do a lot for your self-esteem, whatever qualitative improvements you feel you have made. For many, an IQ score purports to be evidence, or validation, of intelligence. So, although far from the full intelligence story, in Chapter 2 you will learn how to increase your IQ score. In the other chapters, you will learn to improve other types of intelligence from those described in Chapter 1.

As it happens, some of the other types of intelligence you will learn about are much more amenable to DIY improvement than IQ. So if, after working through Chapter 2, you can demonstrate an improvement in IQ, this seemingly immutable measure of intelligence, you will have little difficulty with the others.

Each kind of intelligence has different value to an individual and within a culture or environment. Very many mothers-cum-housewives, for instance, have the kind of intelligence to juggle a dozen tasks that many so-called intelligent people, particularly men, could not begin to tackle. The value of any kind of intelligence depends on what you want to do with it, and what is important in your life – your personal world. It's a case of smart horses for smart courses, and that leaves us plenty of choice and opportunity for improvement.

If the experts disagree, who decides on what intelligence is anyway? The teacher or pupil? The employer or employee? The student or the examining body? The salaried, professional manager or the self-employed entrepreneur? The interviewer or the interviewee? The scientist who sees the mind as a machine or the philosopher who sees the ghost in the machine? Answering such questions – even if we could – will help us little if it transpires that intelligence is a genetic trait we are born with and stuck with for life. What hope have we if it turns out we are lumbered with a low intelligence score courtesy of our less-intelligent predecessors?

The question this book addresses is how to be more intelligent *whatever* definition you settle on (within the bounds of common sense, which is one of the definitions anyway). In disagreeing fundamentally, the experts we would expect to be wise in the matter are of little help. However, as we uncover some of the secrets of the brain, you can make your own judgement about intelligence:

- what intelligence means to you;
- what it means to employers, clients, friends, teachers – those who might influence your 'success' and future;
- what you want to do or be through improving your intelligence – what may have motivated you to read this book;
- what particular kinds of intelligence you value, and what you want more of;
- in what ways you would wish to behave differently given your new, improved intelligence;
- how committed you are to living up to the full potential of your intelligence.

Becoming more intelligent may require some *unlearning*. We are creatures of habit, and we don't take well to change in attitudes and behaviour, even when it is for the better. The biggest part is getting to know and use your innate intelligence, in its different forms. Unless you have undergone major brain surgery, you can take it that your brain 'hardware' resources are more than adequate. That's just a fact of neurophysiology. However, a person's brain may atrophy by non-use, ignorance, culture and conditioning. That's where the unlearning, especially of unhelpful self-beliefs and early 'intelligence conditioning', comes into play. Thereafter, with a clean mental slate, it doesn't require superhuman qualities to tap your intelligent mind and rise to your potential. Amazingly, even a person of low 'left-brain' IQ can easily acquire mental 'software', to increase his or her true intelligence, and use it to better purpose.

Your brain can handle far, far more than you might have imagined. It translates into intelligence and, in turn, tangible, meaningful achievements. Intelligence, in its true sense, is your personal key to finding and fulfilling your life purposes.

The bottom line is that intelligence, in just about any guise, is up for grabs. That is good news for the large majority of ordinary people who cluster around average IQ, but *know* they could do better if they set their minds to it. Whereas IQ doesn't correlate to 'success' in a material sense (like salary or bank balance), we shall see that intelligence in its wider senses certainly does. So you can apply your boosted intelligence – of whatever kind – towards a better job, better relationships, wider, more fulfilling interests, and a more satisfying life.

Like most worthwhile things in life, it starts with a decision. Fortunately, making a decision about how to use your brain doesn't require a super brain in the first place – just common sense and a bit of know-how which you can easily pick up as you go along. It means deciding to make the most of your mental resources.

Just knowing what you want, what is important to you, and the sort of things that make you happy – self-awareness if you like – is another basic 'intelligence' trait. And there are ways of setting powerful, motivating goals. Insofar as your genes have a role to play, the decisions you are free to make and the skills you can learn as you read on, play a far bigger role. That means that when it comes to our potential as otherwise ordinary human beings, the playing fields are level. You have the choice to get to know and use your mind to its full potential. To *learn* intelligence.

Some aspects of improving intelligence have been deliberately omitted. It is a big topic, and those areas in which readers can bring about improvements both materially and fairly quickly have been concentrated upon. There is no doubt, for instance, that diet and exercise, which have not been addressed, have an effect on the mind as well as the body. Plenty of research, shows, for instance, that undernourished children do badly on intelligence scores and that exercise right into old age, as well as mental stimulation, can have cognitive benefits. Also not mentioned here is memory as a major factor in intelligence, although it is central to how we think and, in old age especially, is directly correlated to cognitive health. This is partly because it does not figure in the main popular definitions of intelligence which have been used as a working shortlist (out of literally hundreds) for practical purposes and which is introduced in Chapter 1. But memory is also a subject – like exercise and dieting – already well covered, including in some of this author's own books.

In Chapter 1 we consider the question 'what is intelligence?', describe the different kinds of intelligence 'on offer', what each might mean to us, and our potential to develop and improve them. Chapter 2 concentrates on IQ, and specifically shows you how you can increase your IQ score by several points through test-sophistication and practice. Chapters 3 and 4 address two main areas of intelligence – intrapersonal and interpersonal – that form part of 'multiple intelligences' and 'emotional intelligence' (EI, or EQ) which you will first meet in Chapter 1. In Chapter 5, the remaining aspects of EQ are addresssed, and in particular how you can improve this important aspect of your intelligence. In Chapter 6 you will learn some important principles and techniques that are associated with very high intelligence, mastery, and genius. Building on what you will have learnt in earlier chapters, this final intelligence 'masterclass' will show you how you can make extraordinary advances in intelligence and achievement and find greater fulfilment in your life.

1

What intelligence can mean for you

When campaigning against Eisenhower for the American presidency, a supporter encouraged Adlai Stevenson with the remark: 'Governor, every intelligent person will be voting for you.'

'That's not enough,' Stevenson is reported to have replied, 'I need a majority.'

This anecdote says less about the voters than the different meanings we give to 'intelligent'. We mostly agree that not everybody is intelligent to the same level or, in some cases, at all. And most of us know what we mean by an 'intelligent' person. For instance, we might remark about a child being 'very intelligent', and can usually rank work colleagues and acquaintances on a scale of 'very bright' to 'very dim'. We are all experts at spotting 'intelligence'. However, along with the experts, we differ widely as to just what it is and who we think exhibits it.

This chapter will address the question, 'What is intelligence, and what can it mean for you?', and trace its importance over the years. In particular, some of the main types of intelligence that have been identified will briefly be described: IQ, the most common use of the term; EQ (emotional quotient), or EI, (emotional intelligence); and 'multiple intelligences' (MI).

Together, these provide a checklist you can use to decide which kinds of intelligence are important to you, and which you want to develop, improve or perfect.

You may discover you have intelligence that you have never recognized as such. Or there may be some aspects of intelligence on which you rate yourself low, but you can nevertheless imagine the benefit of learning or fostering that intelligence if it were possible. You may want to know more about IQ, which is what most people equate with intelligence, and in particular how you can increase your own score. As you discover multiple intelligences and EQ, intelligence may take on a new meaning, and present opportunities you had not thought of.

Whichever intelligence you 'choose', you can improve it. Indeed, depending on your starting point, and the 'type' of intelligence you choose, you can expect to make changes that will affect your life in remarkable ways. Once you discover what intelligence can mean for you and how you rate yourself, you will then be ready to make the specific changes described in the later chapters, and apply them immediately in your life.

What is intelligence?

When we get down to specifics, we soon realize why the term intelligence is hard to define, let alone measure.

Streetwise savvy

In particular, intelligence seems to depend on the context or environment. For instance, a street child in Rio de Janeiro or Calcutta will make a gullible tourist look decidedly dumb in the child's own, familiar environment. Similarly, a cerebral professor may appear not very intelligent when facing some of the day-to-day practical problems we all encounter.

There is a 'savvy' or 'streetwise' kind of intelligence that seems to be at least as important as intellectual or academic intelligence. However, neither kind of intelligence may display 'wisdom', 'insight', 'understanding', 'perception', 'shrewdness' and a score of other popular meanings ascribed to intelligence. None of these, we shall see, requires a special intelligence birthright. Each lies within your potential. So, to a remarkable degree, you can develop the particular intelligence attributes you want to display in your own life.

Intelligence in the beholder's eye

However we define intelligence, it can have a profound effect on our lives, not least because of what *others* mean by intelligence. Sometimes an intelligence 'score' can pigeonhole us, for instance, into a particular education band. Such was the case in the days of the eleven-plus test which children had to undergo for grammar school selection in the UK. We each have our own understanding of intelligence, and how we rate ourselves. We need to know, however, how it may affect us in different areas of our life, not least through the impact of other people who have their own ideas about intelligence.

For instance, 'intelligence' is often a factor in job selection or promotion. This applies especially when recruitment involves psychometric tests. At the same time, different interviewers will inevitably have their own ideas about intelligence and how to spot it. Or they will have opinions about what kind of intelligence is needed for a particular job, or to match their particular company culture. Like beauty, for better or worse (and with equally serious consequence), intelligence is in the eye of the beholder.

'Intelligence' may be a factor when recruiting a junior shop assistant ('Wanted: intelligent, energetic young...') just as when hiring a management consultant, nurse or chief executive. Its influence is all pervading, and job recruitment is just one example. Intelligence is often a characteristic we look for in our ideal partner, and they in us. It is a key attribute in 'personality' and how we perceive and value each other. It's too important to leave to psychologists to define and measure.

Playing to your mental strengths

There's good and bad news in all of this. The bad news is that, whilst there is no agreement about what intelligence is, Western society nonetheless places great store on IQ, which, at best, reflects some aspects only of intelligence. For better or worse, the IQ lottery can have a life-changing effect on many people. The bad news gets worse, of course, for people lumbered with a low IQ, courtesy of their parents' genes, and about which they can supposedly do nothing.

The good news is that the wide range of 'intelligence' identified and recently popularized, allows many more people to legitimately rank as 'intelligent' in one or more areas of their lives. Better still, there are proven ways to increase different types of intelligence. So we now have some choice as to the kind of intelligence we wish to foster and improve. Put simply, you can choose the kind of intelligence you fancy, 'learn' and perfect it, and apply it to get on better in your life.

In some cases this might just involve playing to your mental strengths (or 'types of intelligence') once you have identified them. Optimizing one's mental powers is a characteristic of smart people anyway. In other cases, it might mean choosing some *latent* intelligence that you want to rekindle and improve, or correcting an intelligence 'blind spot'. In each case you can apply your true intelligence to achieving your present goals and purposes.

Smart horses for smart courses

Some aspects or types of intelligence will have a bigger impact on your life and circumstances than others. As we have seen, IQ may affect your academic attainment and job opportunities.

Artistic or musical intelligence (two examples of 'multiple intelligences') will similarly affect people differently, depending on their goals in life and chosen career. Some types of intelligence have a greater effect on career attainment and 'success' in a material or financial sense. Other kinds of intelligence may contribute more to a sense of personal fulfilment or purpose, or quality of life, however such intelligence is valued by society at large. So it's 'smart horses for smart courses'. Only you can choose. For present purposes you need to understand what intelligence means for *you*, and what it can mean in your life. More specifically, you need a strategy to develop and use.

Take your intelligent pick

There are as many approaches to learning, releasing, stimulating and displaying intelligence as there are definitions. Some intelligence traits are more amenable to ordinary, school-type learning. Others require a different approach and you can't learn them as you would multiplication tables or poetry. Some aspects of intelligence, for example, involve 'left-brain' kinds of activity such as logic and reasoning, whilst others maybe require 'right-brain' aptitudes associated with intuitive, holistic thinking. 'Emotional intelligence', for instance, is a different kind of animal to IQ-type intelligence. At the same time, social, or 'people skills' are less teachable in a conventional, academic sense than verbal and numeric skills. Paradoxically, perhaps, they are more *learnable* in the school of real life, for those actively wanting to learn and improve. Moreover, whether numerically scored or not, there is plenty of room for improvement well beyond teenage years when our conventional IQ is supposed to plateau.

The different kinds of intelligence in your 'intelligence shopping list' have some things in common:

- You need not be stuck with them. In different ways and to different degrees you can *change them for the better*, and improve your 'performance'.
- They can have a real effect on your life, at work, socially and in your family life. They are not scores or labels such as exams you have passed that have little to do with your real life. When you boost your true intelligence, you and others will know the difference.
- You can't isolate them or their effects. They are interdependent and synergistic. Together, these manifestations of intelligence are as close to the real 'you' as any aspect of your personality.

Let's start with a few 'recognized' definitions of intelligence, all of which come with their own pedigree of validity. None, however, is widely accepted as a standard definition.

Some definitions

'An inborn or innate quality, as distinct from abilities acquired through individual experience.'

Encyclopaedia Britannica

'An innate quality, as distinct from abilities acquired through learning.'

Herbert Spencer

'Innate general cognitive ability.'

Cyril Burt

'... capacity to act purposefully, think rationally and deal effectively with the environment.'

D Wechsler

'Intelligence is the ability to face problems in an unprogrammed (creative) manner.'

Stephen J Gould

'... the ability to carry out abstract thinking.'

L M Terman

'The test of a first-rate intelligence is the ability to hold two opposed ideas in mind at the same time and still retain the ability to function.'

F Scott Fitzgerald

'... the ability to pick the appropriate behaviour for situations encountered in an environment.'

Robert Franklin

'Intelligence is the ability to apply existing knowledge to solve new problems; the degree of intelligence is measured by the speed with which the agent solves problems.'

Donald Sterner

So much for definitions. It may be better, however, to ask what is intelligence based on, what makes it, and what traits and characteristics does it comprise of?

What makes intelligence?

In fact, the principles upon which intelligence is understood to be based, and the characteristics it purports to comprise, are as diverse as the definitions. However, British psychologists, Cyril Burt and C E Spearman, both supported two basic principles, maintaining that intelligence is firstly, a single, measurable entity and secondly, innate and unchangeable.

University of Chicago psychologist L L Thurston disagreed, contending that there were seven primary mental abilities:

- verbal comprehension;
- word fluency;
- computational ability;
- spatial visualization;
- associative memory;
- perceptual speed;
- reasoning.

The intelligence free-for-all

Another psychologist, Joy P Guilford, identified no less than *120* types of mental ability. Then Stephen J Gould, a contemporary Harvard scientist and prolific science author, maintained that intelligence cannot adequately be measured. The very fact that estimates of the number of primary abilities have ranged from Thurston's 7 to Guilford's 120 or more indicates that vectors of mind may be figments of mind.

The intelligence free-for-all continues. As recently as the 1990s, John B Carroll has suggested more than 70 different abilities that can be identified in IQ scores.

A majority view

Insofar as there is any majority view, 52 mainstream psychologists signed a statement, published in the *Wall Street Journal* in December 1994, contending that:

- Intelligence exists as a very general mental capability involving ability to reason, plan, solve problems, think abstractly, comprehend complex ideas, learn quickly and learn from cxpcricncc.
- Intelligence can be measured, and IQ tests measure it well. Non-verbal tests can be used where language skills are weak.
- IQ tests are not culturally biased.
- IQ is more strongly related than any other measurable human trait to educational, economic, occupation and

social outcomes. Whatever it is that IQ tests measure, it is very important.

- Genetics plays a bigger role than environment in intelligence, but environment has a strong effect.
- Individuals are not born with an unchangeable IQ, but it gradually stabilizes during childhood and changes little thereafter.

It would be interesting to obtain such a collective statement of tenets from 52 businesspeople, housewives, politicians or teenagers. Almost certainly those statements would add to the rich diversity of meaning that intelligence generates. And almost certainly they would confirm that no *single* definition of intelligence is acceptable for any serious use of the term. As it is, the prestigious *Wall Street Journal* statement says as much about contemporary psychologists and predominant Western culture as it does about intelligence.

Another major attempt at a consensus definition of intelligence was made at a symposium in which the editors of the *Journal of Educational Psychology* asked those prominent in the area of intelligence testing what they considered 'intelligence' to be. The great diversity of answers prompted E G Boring to remark, half-jokingly, that 'intelligence is what intelligence tests test'.

Intelligence and the environment

In fact, the diversity of meaning that intelligence evokes is even greater than the hundreds of definitions, attempted over the centuries, at first suggest. Not surprisingly, most of the definitions fall somewhere in the nature-nurture categories of intelligence – are we born with it (nature) or do we acquire it through our environment (nurture)? However, if the concept of intelligence is taken back to basics it raises principles that go even deeper than the ubiquitous nature-nurture question. Consider the following, for instance.

Inanimate things

Inanimate objects of the mineral kingdom like stones and water do not act by themselves on the environment. When they move it is because something else moves them. Not much intelligence there. The exception is man-made mechanisms, such as motor-cars, microwave ovens and automatic pilots in airliners. These act according to objectives, albeit objectives set by people rather than the inanimate objects themselves. This can *appear* like intelligent behaviour, especially in the case of advanced robotics. But otherwise the inanimate world has a very low mental age. It doesn't score well on intelligence tests.

The plant kingdom

Plants have the decided advantage over sand and stones by being alive, so how do they fare in the intelligence stakes? They act on the environment in certain situations, such as when they bend towards a light source and their roots grow towards moisture. In this case plants seem to have built-in 'objectives' (tendencies, attraction) towards which they move. Compared with the mineral world – say stones being washed down a canyon – plant tricks are fairly impressive. However, plant behaviour of this sort is 'pre-programmed'. The plant doesn't *learn* anything. It doesn't add capability by virtue of *experience*. In fact, after millennia of practice at photosynthesis, even the prettiest plants seem hopelessly dumb. In fairness, however, a blade of grass somehow comes across as brighter than a lump of sandstone.

The animal kingdom

Although animals get around better than plants, and much better than stones, much of their behaviour is instinctive and reactive. Like plants, an animal is biologically pre-programmed. So, however remarkable its behaviour, even from the moment of birth, it doesn't seem to apply much thought or intelligence to its feats. Only where an animal appears to *learn from experience* (which plants don't seem to aspire to) do scientists start to impute intelligence to the lower animal kingdom (except when besotted with their own domestic pets).

Learning for an intelligent purpose

The ability to learn, therefore, would seem to be an important threshold when considering the basics of intelligence. This applies widely in the animal world. An animal tries out different actions in different situations and remembers (if it survives) whether they help or hinder. The 'objective' in this case is usually to gain pleasure and avoid pain. More fundamentally, to survive. Such learning seems passive and instinctive. Learning, *in order to better achieve a self-set objective*, however, seems the kind that takes us further up the ladder of intelligence. Not surprisingly, 'purposeful learning' figures large in any definition of human intelligence.

Pain/pleasure/survival behaviour is also common in humans, of course. We also prefer pleasure to pain, given the choice. However, this can be in a dimension not found in the lower animals. Pleasure, for instance, may be more than just physical. A person can get pleasure from solving a problem, feeling a task has been well done, or knowing that the weekend is about to start. Importantly, we can gain pleasure in achieving a *self-imposed* objective. In other words, we can act with a purpose, and gain pleasure in succeeding in that purpose. That seems to be a key ingredient of the higher intelligence we are interested in understanding, improving and applying.

Getting back to basics gets us away from the narrow and patently Western notion of intelligence. But, unfortunately, even with 'learning' and 'purpose', intelligence is no easier to pin down. We all have different goals and objectives, and use our intelligence to achieve all manner of subjective, individualistic purposes. Not only do we pursue different goals, but also we do this in as many different ways, and with different motives. If you like, we have different behavioural strategies. Intelligence seems to be the extent to which these behavioural strategies succeed in achieving our (specific, individual, self-set) purpose. Put another way, what intelligence *does* is more relevant than what it *is*. Seen in this light, intelligence matches some of the definitions we met earlier: the measure of whether we can solve problems, gain pleasure, survive. In short, the extent to which we achieve our purposes. We can put it this way:

It's smart to consistently achieve what you set out to achieve, using whatever knowledge, experience, talents or skills you can call upon.

Whilst learning and intent (or purpose) seem to be key to intelligence, *how and what we learn and how we choose our purposes* are not so clear. No surprise, then, that Guilford identified 120 human intelligences. No surprise that we can all spot intelligence, and the lack of it, all around us even though we would be hard-pressed to define it.

Quick thinking

There are enormous differences in the speed and efficiency of learning. One of the definitions listed earlier referred to 'the speed [at] which the agent solves problems'. Animals learn better than plants and human beings learn much better than the lower animals. However, there is wide variation, and clever animals often seem more intelligent than stupid humans. Similarly, any normal, healthy small child appears intelligent ('gifted' to his or her parents), irrespective of the subject they are learning and despite their relatively small fund of knowledge and experience. In their seemingly insatiable capacity for learning they leave knowledgeable, but relatively sluggard, grown-up learners far behind. Their 'intelligence' seems to increase by the hour and knows no bounds. They learn *quickly*, and that seems to be a hallmark of childhood intelligence.

Fortunately, we can do a lot to improve the speed and efficiency of our learning, even though we can't change the mechanics of how our brain does these things (which we don't understand anyway). Many of the pioneering scientific experiments into intelligence involved speed of response in otherwise simple motor movements, or 'reaction time'. That aspect of intelligence, which we see in driving a car or playing squash, can be improved with practice and eventually becomes habitual – we do it 'without thinking'. Children mastering computer games requiring fast reaction display such apparently superintelligence. However, these child prodigies – a generation of them – are not necessarily ten times as intelligent as their bewildered elders. They learn fast because they don't have the inhibitions and negative self-beliefs of grown-ups, and they enjoy it. They soon become practice-perfect. Or maybe older sluggards, insofar as they still fall short of Junior even after trying hard and practice, are simply less intelligent *in that kind of intelligence*, more likely, in that specific application (like computer games). But even oldies can improve, and that's what matters. Speed of thinking (given a limited lifespan) is an important variable in some types of intelligence.

Speed and efficiency do not always equate with intelligence, however. Sometimes a slower, more thorough approach, combined with will power and perseverance, is the smart way to achieve a particular purpose. In any case, *outputs* rather than *inputs* (whether mental 'trying' or physical effort) are what count. In other words, true intelligence is more to do with results.

One more definition seems to capture this aspect of intelligence:

The comparative level of performance (effectiveness) of a system in reaching its own objectives.

Effectiveness in achieving objectives is a feature of human intelligence. Reaching objectives *more often* and *more quickly* – that is, more effectively – demonstrates higher intelligence, whatever form behaviour takes. Not only can we identify and use otherwise latent intelligence, but we can use it more efficiently and to greater effect.

Measuring intelligence

The absence of any accepted definition of intelligence should be sufficient grounds for caution whenever we consider any kind of intelligence measurement, whether purporting to be scientific or not. Not only have definitions varied over time, but they have also varied between experts at any time. To this day there remains a wide divergence of opinions and no small passion on the part of intelligence pundits. Advances in neurophysiology and brain-scanning technology only raise further questions as the awesome complexity of the brain is revealed. With each scientific advance, the extent of human intelligence becomes ever more elusive, but that has not hindered the pseudoscience of intelligence measurement.

Intelligence measuring started with Sir Francis Galton. He was keen on measuring just about everything, so intelligence inevitably had its turn. Inspired by his cousin Charles Darwin, he saw intelligence as a biological factor. His motley, ingenious experiments measured his student subjects on physical strength, such as handgrip, reaction time, speed of hand motion, judgements of length and such like. Not surprisingly, he found great differences in 'intelligence'. These he attributed to differences in natural ability, or the 'indication of superior strains and races'. In fact, we now know that his measurements simply reflected contemporary views about education, race and class. Nonetheless, the obsession with measuring intelligence continues in the form of IQ.

One hundred years of IQ

IQ usually comes to mind when we think about intelligence, and especially intelligence measurement. Although it is well entrenched in Western education and culture, there is little agreement as to how effective IQ tests are in measuring true intelligence. Regardless of the many types of intelligence that IQ does *not* measure, even those that it purports to measure take on a different meaning in different cultures. For this reason, no test is 'culture free'. Nonetheless, IQ tests are a major factor in education and job selection, as we saw earlier, and for various academic and professional entrance requirements.

Alfred Binet developed the first intelligence test for school children in Paris between 1905 and 1911. 'Intelligence quotient' was born after his work was translated into English at Stanford University in America and adapted by psychologist L M Terman as the Stanford–Binet test. This IQ test, widely revised over the years, is the one most commonly used.

IQ measures how an individual performs on an intelligence test as compared with the rest of the population. Initially, 'intelligence' was largely verbal, and later numerical and visual–spatial skills were included. Average intelligence is 100, and a lower or higher IQ figure reflects a lower or higher intelligence.

IQ uses the concept of mental age. A child that performs on tests to the level of the average ten-year-old is said to have a mental age of 10, reflecting a bright 8-year-old, say, or a not-so-bright 12-year-old. It was found that mental age stops advancing somewhere between the ages of 14 and 18 years, at which an adult IQ applies for the rest of your life.

'Natural inequality'

The idea of intelligence has been linked to social and political ideals throughout history, and this persists in IQ. The concept of 'natural inequality', for instance, became popular in the nineteenth century with new social alignments at home and colonialism abroad. Some argued that colonial exploitation was justified because 'the minds of the inferior human races cannot respond to relations of everyday mediocrity'. The poor, having proved themselves to be 'unfit', should be denied all social welfare and allowed to die off. A 'scientific' measure of intelligence, easily correlated to poor education and economic circumstances (*inter alia*), made this ideal a practical reality.

Unlike most scientific concepts, once accepted, IQ has been particularly dogged with dogma and controversy. The pioneers were strong hereditarians and eugenicists who used IQ to support their cause, without being too scrupulous of the scientific validity of the tests. Some supporters held explicitly racist, eugenicist and pro-Nazi views.

Feeblemindedness

Remarkably, IQ to this day is used as a social and political tool and has been the centre of some of the biggest controversies in psychology and education. Lewis Terman translated Binet's test in 1916 to be used as a means of identifying 'mental defectives'. His idea was to clear the streets of 'feeblemindedness' (the term for mental disability in the USA at the time), thus eliminating 'crime, pauperism and industrial inefficiency'. His contemporary, Henry H Goddard, argued along similar lines that feebleminded people must not be allowed to reproduce, and used the IQ test as a crucial instrument in his propaganda. It was applied in particular to justify stemming the tide of immigrants into the USA. Goddard betrays blatant unscientific, non-objective methods when he states:

'After a person has had considerable experience in this work, he almost gets a sense of what a feebleminded person is so that he can tell one afar off.'

Through the powerful tool of a 'scientific' intelligence test, he informed fellow Americans that 83 per cent of Hungarians, 79 per cent of Italians, and 87 per cent of Russians were feebleminded. Psychologists, ranking low in comparison to the 'hard' scientists, warmed to these ideas with so many practical benefits and pressed for immigration controls, which eventually become law in 1924.

The subsequent growth of the IQ movement was openly racist. Followers of Terman and Goddard advocated sterilizing the feebleminded, on the basis of a half-hour written test, culturally biased to white, middle-class Anglo Saxons and the prevailing educational traditions. Many American states took up their policies. Tens of thousands of surgical operations were carried out. IQ was hailed as an accurate measure of the 'genetic worth' of people. The views fuelled eugenic ideas in many countries, including Britain. Karl Pearson's piece in the prestigious *Encyclopaedia Britannica* reads:

'It is cruel to the individual; it serves no social purpose, to drag a man of only moderate intellectual power from the hand-working to the brain-working group.'

A report to the Board of Education in 1911 recommended the use of IQ tests for the identification of 'defectives'. This report was the foundation of the 'eleven-plus' examination and the selective state schooling system that affected the lives of millions of children. The same ideology was affecting lives in Nazi Germany in an even more fundamental way.

Predicting success

In fact, IQ tests do have validity within certain limits. In particular, they have been able to predict academic success, and success in getting the sort of jobs, such as in the professions and higher education, that require academic qualifications. However, they have been less successful predictors of performance *in* those jobs, or longer-term career success. Their validity, moreover, only applies within the culture from which the tests have arisen, and (hardly surprising) when the test language is in the subject's mother tongue.

More cynically, IQ tests have been seen as a good measure of *the skill needed to do well in IQ tests*. This is no surprise, of course, as the tests themselves reflect their own culture, educational ideals and traditions, and the kind of things we learn at school. Questions such as 'In what continent is Egypt?', 'Who wrote Hamlet?' and 'What is the boiling point of water?', for example, seem to demand more than the right genes. Such questions are certainly not culture-free.

Interestingly, teachers themselves have predicted, with far greater accuracy, the future achievements of their pupils. Yet, rather disconcertingly, the IQ test lives on, enmeshed in the educational, social and political mêlée of each generation. For whatever reason, IQ-type intelligence, and all it connotes, is alive and well. For our present purposes, it is simply a measure of one particular kind of intelligence, the characteristics of which (such as verbal and numerical skills) can be improved. Chapter 2 shows you how you can increase your IQ score.

Multiple intelligences

Howard Gardner and a team of researchers at Harvard University popularized the idea of multiple intelligences. He identified seven types of intelligence, and more recently an eighth and a ninth (which, however, are not yet fully paid-up MI members and subject to further research). The next section gives brief descriptions of Gardner's multiple intelligence categories. Ask yourself:

- Have I got this kind of intelligence?
- Did I have it when I was younger?
- Have I looked on this as intelligence?

- Have I lost any of these sorts of skills, perhaps by not using them?
- How might I improve in one or more of these intelligence categories?
- How would I like to apply my intelligence?

These are important questions if you are to develop your true intelligence to the full.

Verbal–linguistic intelligence

This is responsible for language and everything that stems from reading and writing. It embraces storytelling, metaphors and similes, abstract reasoning, humour, symbolic thinking and such like. We witness such intelligence in writers, poets, playwrights, public speakers and comedians. Verbal–linguistic ability is a well-accepted criterion for intelligence and forms part of any orthodox IQ test. It clearly puts at a disadvantage those whose first language is other than the test language. Insofar as it demands a grasp of the language and vocabulary, verbal-linguistic intelligence is affected by ordinary schooling and in particular reading experience – neither of which are genetic factors. So even this core component of an IQ test cannot restrict itself to measuring innate, or natural intelligence characteristics.

Logical–mathematical intelligence

This is associated with inductive reasoning, or 'scientific' thinking. It includes the capacity to work with numbers and other symbols, and to see relationships between separate bits of information. We observe this sort of intelligence typically in scientists, accountants, computer programmers, bankers, lawyers and mathematicians. Logical–mathematical intelligence is another of the core components of standard IQ tests and is covered more fully in Chapter 2. Together with verbal-linguistic intelligence, these form the basis of Western education and much academic attainment.

Visual–spatial intelligence

This deals with the visual arts such as painting, drawing and sculpture and disciplines such as navigation, map making and architecture, which require an ability to use space and 'imagine' spatial relationships. It involves forming mental images, and the ability to imagine objects from different perspectives. It crops up in many mental competencies and traits, from spelling to self-motivation and creative problem solving.

Bodily–kinaesthetic intelligence

This form of intelligence is the ability to use the body to express emotion, such as in dance, sports and physical games, and also 'body language' when communicating. It also includes skills such as riding a bike, swimming and driving a car, which require 'muscle memory'. Specifically, it involves physical dexterity that does not demand 'conscious' thinking, and which, after practice, becomes automatic. We see it, for example, in actors, athletes and dancers, and inventors. It usually appears as a 'gift', or special talent, however much the individual has studied, practised and persevered to achieve mastery.

Musical–rhythmic intelligence

This includes the ability to recognize rhythmic and tonal patterns and sensitivity to sounds in the environment, especially the human voice and musical instruments. We see this sort of intelligence in musicians and music teachers and also advertisers who use catchy tunes to sell their products. These auditory sensitivities have a great effect on consciousness and emotion, as in the effect of great music, the simplest tune that recalls a vivid memory, or a rhythm that seems to reach to our very bones. Sensitivity to the human voice is typical of good listeners, and is an important aspect of interpersonal communication.

Intrapersonal intelligence

This form of intelligence ('intra' meaning within) focuses on the self and concerns what we generally call self-knowledge. It is associated with refection, awareness and control of emotions, intuition and spiritual awareness. It involves consciousness, 'self' or 'identity', and thinking processes themselves – thinking about thinking. It sometimes includes objectivity, and the ability to stand back and see things from another perspective, as well as to be able to identify and express in language subjective thoughts and feelings. It can extend to include what is termed 'higher consciousness', in which we contemplate and visualize what is possible, who we are, and the bigger question of the meaning of life. Although not identified with particular professions, as are visual skills in artists, we see evidence of this kind of intelligence in philosophers, psychiatrists, mystics and spiritual counsellors. Intrapersonal intelligence, and how you can improve it, is covered in more detail in Chapter 3.

Interpersonal intelligence

This involves the ability to work in co-operation with other people and communicate well both verbally and non-verbally ('inter' meaning among or between). A person with this kind of intelligence will notice moods, temperament, motivations and intentions in others. We sometimes term this empathy, or a feeling for how others feel. It means understanding people's fears, hopes and beliefs. Being able to 'read' other people is an important aspect of the 'social intelligence' we see demonstrated in counsellors, teachers, therapists, politicians, religious leaders and successful managers. Interpersonal intelligence, and how you can improve it, is covered in more detail in Chapter 4.

Gardner's multiple intelligences, once understood, are not difficult to recognize, both in ourselves, and in people we meet. They are not either/or characteristics. The fact is that we all have all these intelligences, and display them in different ways and to different degrees in our work and personal lives. Clearly, some types of intelligence have a higher value in certain jobs and situations, such as interpersonal skills in selling, teaching and counselling, and visual–spatial skills in architecture. Each type of intelligence can be developed and improved by training, such as in accountancy or engineering, and by lengthy practice such as in music or athletics. The scope for improvement will vary from intelligence to intelligence, and from person to person. Each of us, in turn, will apply or use our portfolio of multiple intelligences in different ways and with different degrees of success.

Unlike IQ, none of Gardner's types of intelligence, whatever part genetics plays in them, purports to remain fixed from teenage. So, not only do you have lots of scope in the kinds of intelligence you would like to display, but also in the level you want to attain. You can keep learning, and keep growing in intelligence.

Emotional intelligence

As we have seen, IQ has gained much credence over the years and is now well embedded in our Western educational tradition. Once stripped of its political overtones, it is fine – as far as it goes. However, as we have seen, it doesn't go much farther than the classroom, and rarely outside the academic and scientific worlds in which verbal, numerical skills are particularly valued. In the world most of us know, you need other kinds of resourcefulness, and in particular the 'people skills' that largely constitute interpersonal intelligence.

The biggest thing to hit the intelligence community since IQ is EQ – *emotional* intelligence – the *emotional* equivalent of cognitive IQ. Emotional intelligence is a relatively new term, but a familiar enough concept under different labels. It now has an all-pervading influence and, in particular, better reflects the kinds of intelligence that most people need to call upon most of the time in modern life. It makes more 'sense', as we understand more about the nature of intelligence. It is a better predictor of 'success' as it is most commonly defined, such as in career or monetary terms.

There is much about EQ that sounds like common sense, so it is not surprising it has caught the popular imagination. Isn't it obvious that to be able to show empathy or to control anger, for instance, is likely to be a better predictor of success than the kind of abstract intelligence measured by IQ?

The five domains of emotional intelligence

EQ includes some of the multiple intelligences we have already met, and in particular embraces the intra- and inter-personal intelligences. Five domains are usually cited:

- knowing your emotions;
- managing your emotions;
- motivating yourself;
- recognizing emotion in others;
- handling relationships.

In particular, EQ involves 'people skills', and the emotional strengths that we need to do well in life regardless of our educational attainments and IQ score. As we have seen, many different kinds of intelligence have been identified and these all have an effect on the outcomes of our lives. And whilst some would question the degree to which we can improve our IQ score (although you will learn in the next chapter how to do just that), there is plenty of scope for improving aspects of our emotional intelligence. This particularly applies to those aspects that may have been neglected due to low self-image, or have lain dormant through non-use. These are likely to show big improvements as we reclaim our true intelligence. These, in turn, are the 'social competencies' that tend to have the biggest effect on our everyday lives.

Emotion versus cognition

Emotion, as such, does not figure heavily in Gardner's seven intelligences. Even in what can be described as his personal intelligences ('intrapersonal' and 'interpersonal') he emphasizes *cognition*, or understanding of oneself and others. The emphasis is on being *aware* of emotions, in a conscious, rational way, rather than just *feeling* them or *expressing* them.

However, aspects of emotion seem beyond the reach of language and cognition, and the conscious mind. That's what makes emotion, and that's what makes emotional intelligence important. EQ includes the ability to express emotion, an awareness and understanding of it, and the ability to regulate and control it.

Two Americans, Peter Salovey (Yale) and John Mayer (New Hampshire) coined the term emotional intelligence. It has its roots in 'social intelligence', first identified by E L Thorndyke in 1920. Schoolteachers have used the rudiments of EI since the 1970s under labels such as 'social development' and 'personal intelligence'.

Mayer defined EQ as:

a group of mental abilities which help you recognize and understand your own feelings and others' which leads to the ability to regulate your feelings.

There are two sides to emotional intelligence. You need your intellect to understand emotion. You need your emotional mind to add creativity and intuition to your logical mind. Neither is an easy proposition for humans. On the one hand, emotions sometimes get the better of our rational minds, and seem to dictate our behaviour if not run our lives – or at best limit our potential. On the other hand, the emotional mind, associated with the brain's limbic system and right cortex, often plays second fiddle to the conscious, 'articulate', rational left brain. Intelligence involves both sides of the brain and, even at its highest level, may involve the conflict between 'heart and mind', intuitive and logical thinking. Emotional intelligence calls on holistic, intuitive skills associated with the unconscious part of the mind – the other side of the IQ coin.

In its popular form, EQ has taken on a life of its own and covers a multitude of emotions, traits and personality characteristics. However, John Mayer considered it an *intellectual* skill, just as Howard Gardner did his intrapersonal intelligence. That is, it's not just having feelings, but understanding what they mean. Seeing yourself as if from outside yourself, or as others see you. Such intelligence comes into play when we cognitively, consciously regulate our emotions to achieve some purpose. We will cover EQ in more depth in Chapter 5.

You can now start to decide on your own meaning of intelligence, and think about how it may affect your life. As you read on, rate yourself according to the different kinds of intelligence you will meet and decide in which areas you want to improve your mental skills.

2

Boosting your IQ

In Chapter 1 you learnt about IQ, what it does and doesn't mean in terms of true intelligence. In this chapter you will learn how to improve your score on IQ tests.

There are three main categories of test question:

- verbal;
- numerical;
- visual–spatial.

You can increase your IQ score in two main ways. Firstly, by improving your test-taking skills and practice, or 'test sophistication'. In other words, by getting know-how in the sort of intelligence required to take psychometric tests. Within the above three categories the same sorts of question come up again and again – just as it was in school exams. So you don't need to reinvent the wheel. Simple systems and techniques will soon make what at first seems baffling merely routine. As with any valuable achievement, you just need to *know*. It's up to you whether, and to what extent, you use your intelligence-improving knowledge. Test-taking skills and practice in each area will enable you to increase your IQ by several points.

The second way to improve your score is by adding to your

knowledge and skills in the subject categories of the test. This will mean *learning* from where you left off in the subject, perhaps from school days, and maybe *relearning* what you have forgotten. It's no different from taking up night school or job training in a subject you fancy, to brush up your education. At the end of each section, some 'top scoring tips' in test-taking skills and subject knowledge are given.

How much can you improve your IQ through such ordinary (though perhaps late-in-life) learning? According to IQ purists, once you get past teenage, zero – that's it. You've either got it or you haven't. This author says the reverse: that there is no practical limit to an individual's 'intelligence'. That includes literacy and numeracy, but, as we shall see, it applies to far more than these particular, cognitive uses of the mind.

Beyond test-taking skills, which produce an across-the-board improvement, there is different scope for improvement in these three subject areas. You can improve most in the verbal area, and least in visual–spatial intelligence. That's because each is culture-contaminated to a different level. Verbal intelligence questions are heavily contaminated, not least because they require a good grasp of the test language, culture and general knowledge of the sort we pick up at school and through normal life experience. As you would expect, simply by reading more, and increasing your vocabulary, you can boost this part of your intelligence score.

Numerical questions are not so 'contaminated', but they do require basic arithmetic skills and familiarity with numbers that similarly comes from conventional education and work experience. The visual–spatial questions are as near to culture free as most IQ tests manage to get, so in this third category, most of your improvement will come from test sophistication.

This chapter mainly concentrates on test sophistication, although learning guidelines in the verbal area (where there is plenty of scope for subject intelligence improvement) are given at the end of each of the three test sections. There are plenty of sources for conventional, '3 Rs' learning – such as 'Maths for

Dummies', 'Enjoying Numbers', 'Brush Up Your English' and so on. Test taking know-how, on the other hand, is not so easy to come by, so your learning is fairly self-contained in this chapter.

Test sophistication skills

Let's start with this rather special kind of intelligence: the 'intelligence required to take intelligence tests' – or, more specifically, conventional IQ tests. It is akin to knowing and playing the 'system', which applies in many areas of life. We can call this 'playing the IQ game', and there are some basic requirements:

- Become familiar with the nature of the questions – you can do without surprises. Familiarity will give you confidence so that you are less likely to get stuck and experience mental blocks.
- Learn the principles that apply to most psychometric tests of this sort.
- Learn the methods and techniques to answer different types of question – the know-how.
- Practice, just as with any skill, so that you can answer questions quickly and instinctively.

We can call this test sophistication. In fact, if you haven't carried out this sort of test before, or for many years, it doesn't require much sophistication to substantially improve your score. Before considering specific test questions, some further background to IQ tests and the principles that underlie them will be helpful.

Culture contamination

IQ tests are usually designed to be culture free. However, that is rare in practice. You will meet questions that require straightforward knowledge of word meanings – sometimes subtle meanings. These don't so much depend on 'raw' intelligence, than on education, experience, and exposure to the culture and language. We are stuck with this, and for present purposes, you just need to be aware of it. As we have seen, IQ tests only address a part of what we have identified as intelligence, so what seems an unfair scoring need not be a big deal in practice. As we saw earlier, the more tests demand nurtured (rather than innate) intelligence, the more scope we have for improving it by *more nurture*. In other words, by learning to be more intelligent – where we started. Your first lesson in joined-up intelligence is not to be dumb enough to get yourself scored on intelligence without getting to know what it means and what you can do about it.

Speed matters

How fast do you need to work? Being able to answer questions at speed is a great advantage and is usually part of the test. In some cases the average scorer may not get to finish all the questions. By going faster, whilst still getting the answers right, you will make time for the questions that are particularly difficult, so you will be less anxious through time pressure. Speed comes with familiarity and practice, of course, which is what this chapter is about.

Test-taking mental practice

To become familiar with the various, recurring types of question you don't just need to know the categories (analogies, 'odd one out', etc), but also to have had plenty of practice in answering *actual* questions. Just like doing physical fitness exercises, there is really no shortcut for mental practice. The more your test-taking skills become instinctive, the faster you will work and the more confident you will be. Once you are familiar with a question pattern, only the 'content' of questions will be new. Otherwise the same categories appear again and again.

No tricks

There are no tricks in recognized IQ tests, other than that questions are sometimes specifically couched in a way that the *type of question* is unclear. So by identifying the type quickly, you will save a lot of time and substantially increase your score. That means that if you cannot spot the sort of question you are dealing with ('what on earth does it mean?'), it may be wise to pass on to the next one. This way you can be sure that if you do run out of time, you will omit the trickier questions rather than those you could easily have answered with a bit more time.

Getting chance on your side

Many questions are in effect multiple answer questions, in that you have to choose, say the 'odd one out', from a list of words. That means that the laws of probability operate and you have, perhaps, a one-in-five chance of getting the right answer just by a random guess. The lesson is obvious: always attempt such questions. Over the whole test, your score improvement could be significant. You may meet logical reasoning questions that require a true/false answer, which is better still. At 50/50, these are pretty good odds. Chance plays a part in other ways, and you will learn more about this as you meet specific questions.

Verbal reasoning

Verbal reasoning is the first IQ subject category. Questions can be divided into several types such as 'find the word that fits' and 'analogies', and you will cover all of these. You will not usually be told the type of question, as that is part of the intelligence test. So this is one of the important ways you can prepare for a test, and score higher. You don't *have* to recognize the kind of question, but it may help if you do, as each kind lends itself to a method of answering. Indeed, by spotting the kind of question, you may be more than half way to a solution. At the same time, by knowing what to look for, you will not spend time with trial and error guesses and, worse still, getting stuck and anxious. Familiarity with the various kinds of question – which recur in any popular test – will take the heat out of all but the trickiest.

The verbal reasoning part of an IQ test is particularly 'culture contaminated'. That means that you will require a degree of familiarity with the culture in which the questions are based, and the *language* in which the test is set. Consequently, people who are taking a test in a second language, and are unfamiliar with western education and culture, however intelligent they are, will be at a disadvantage. Conversely, a person taking the test in his or her mother tongue, who is a product of a western education system and a keen reader, will have a decided advantage (again whatever genes this person boasts).

Test your verbal reasoning

Let's make a start at the verbal reasoning part of the test.

Find the odd one out

In this type of question you are given a few words, all but one of which have something in common. You are asked to find the one word that does not belong.

For example:

Find the word that does not belong:

lion tiger elephant horse canary zebra

Solution: canary. (It is a bird and all the others are mammals.)

In this case the categories are animals, birds, etc. They might have been towns and rivers or nouns and verbs – any logical grouping of 'things'. This type of question is straightforward and easy to identify. It will contain the words 'do not belong' or something similar. That is your label to identify the type of question. Nor should it be difficult to spot the common category – 'animal' in the above case. The only real test is therefore to spot the odd one out, and, having got this far, that is easy.

As with any general knowledge type question, you will call upon your vocabulary, experience and interests when doing word-type tests (that is the culture bias that has already been referred to). However, don't overestimate the need for a wide vocabulary. If you don't know what one of the words means, you only have to be sure that all the others fall into the same group to know that the unfamiliar word must be the odd one out. If you spot a word that doesn't belong anyway, you can similarly get away with not knowing the meaning of every other word – you only need one odd one out.

Here's another example of this type:

Find the word that does not belong:

hope love affection envy admiration

Solution: envy. (All the other words are positive emotions.)

Chunks

The common category in this question (emotion, feelings) is not as tangible as 'animals', 'birds' and 'things'. However, the process is the same, and you just need to have an open mind for any kind of grouping. Then, even when you spot it, keep *thinking*. At first sight the words all seem to be emotions, or feelings. However, none of the words seems not to belong. The trick here is to 'chunk' down. To explain this, the previous 'animals' question needs to be referred to. If all the words had been animals (no odd one out), you would then have had to look for a *category* or *example* of animal, which may have been mammals, reptiles, primates or whatever. That is, a smaller logical 'chunk' – and so on down to categories of reptile, categories of lizard and so on, any of which might apply in a question. The presence of a bird makes the previous question easy, but you will often need to test each lower 'chunk', or grouping for an odd one out.

In the 'emotions' question, because all the words seem to be emotions (no odd one out), you need to chunk down to *kinds* of or *examples* of emotion. A negative among positive emotions provides the odd one out.

Twists

Be ready for twists that require just a little more thought.

Look at the following words:

engine Othello noun animal madam

Whilst it may be clear that this is a 'doesn't belong' 'odd one out' type of question, no category of meaning is apparent. That's obvious, so don't spend time thinking of obscure relationships (remember, as a rule there are no tricks). The absence of a common feature is your cue to consider different *sorts* of common feature. Consider, for instance, the words themselves – as a string of letters, if you like – rather than their meanings. For instance, letters common to each word, length of word, grammatical type (verb, noun, etc) and so on.

In this case, all the words except 'animal' start and finish with the same letter. So in this case, *word construction* is the differentiating factor.

Solution: animal. (The other words start and finish with the same letter.)

This is where practice pays off. You only need to have done a specific type of question once or twice before for it to register instinctively as a type of question, such as 'odd one out'.

Checklists

Any technique that will speed up the answering process is valuable, especially if it can be applied to different types of questions. A checklist of 'word construction' features, for instance, would help you to quickly identify the common feature in the previous question. For example:

- number of letters;
- start with the same letter;
- end with the same letter;
- comprise certain kinds of letter (say vowels or consonants);
- 'above and below' construction (lower case letters that extend upwards, eg 'hlbd', and those that extend downwards, eg 'ygjq');
- number of syllables;
- order of the letters, such as alphabetical, reverse alphabetical;
- order of vowels and consonants.

For example, using your checklist method:

Find the odd one out:

first defunct patience hijack stupid

The complete absence of any common meaning alerts you to consider the words as words, regardless of their meaning. You can then expect one of the types in your word construction checklist to apply, which it does: in this case the order of the letters.

Solution: patience. (All the others contain three letters in alphabetical order: 'rst', 'def', 'hij', 'stu'.)

A checklist will cover the majority of questions you will meet, so it is worth using them. However, never assume you have covered all possibilities. Allow your intuitive mind to work for a few moments if your logical checklist doesn't work. Having said that, another tip is just as valuable: don't assume either that a question is 'very hard' (it never is once you solve it!) or that it is a trick, or unfair. You can improve your IQ scores a long way before you need be concerned about such questions.

Time tip

Where there are five or six words in the list, checking the first three will be a sufficient first test. You can expect at least two common features in the first three words (as one of them might be the odd one). You don't therefore need to check all the words. Better to pass on, and try for other possible common features – again testing a couple of words only. This will save time.

In the 'patience' example above, an alphabetical order check would have quickly found 'rst', and 'def' in the next word looks decidedly promising. The next word doesn't fit, but, as the odd word, it needn't. In no more than a second or two you will put the question to bed.

Word sounds

A further twist might have been the sound of the word. For instance, 'dough', 'row', 'toe', 'sew', and 'know' rhyme. 'Bough' or 'cough', in such a list, would be the odd one out. This is an example of knowledge of both spellings and pronunciation (as well as meanings) of English vocabulary masquerading as 'innate' intelligence in a 'culture-free' IQ test.

Analogies

These verbal questions are about relationships. As with the 'odd one out' questions, you need to consider the precise meanings of words, have a good grasp of the language, and be able to distinguish subtle meanings. Let's start with an easy one:

Hand is to **glove** as **foot** is to:

stocking	floor	shoestring	shoe

Solution: stocking.

Don't jump at the first feasible match. In this case 'shoe' seems fine, but a little extra thought will make 'stocking' the best fit (in every sense).

Now try this:

Clock is to **time** as **thermometer** is to:

heat	fever	temperature	humidity

This is trickier. Think before you answer. You can start by elimination, so humidity goes at once. You may find that with practice you develop your own systems for these sorts of question. 'Is to' (in the standard wording of these questions) may not make the relationship clear at all so you may need to apply your own replacement wording. For instance, what about 'clock' *measures* time, or *tells the* time, or *records* time. By testing each word in slightly different ways that express the relationship, it is usually easy to find the correct word, even without working out a precise relationship (which can hurt your brain). However, it pays in these cases to *check every word*. In this case 'thermometer' *measures* heat seems okay until you notice that 'temperature' (which can be hot or cold) fits better. 'Fever' (high or abnormal temperature) is similarly not such a good match. (If you are interested, the instrument for measuring humidity is called a hygrometer.)

Solution: temperature.

Variations can apply here, as with the 'odd one out'. The relationship, for example, may not involve the *meaning*, but the *structure* or some other feature of the word. Try this one:

Star is to **rats** as **ward** is to:

shine mice draw fame

Solution: draw. (Like 'rats' to 'star', 'draw' is 'ward' spelt backwards.)

There is no obvious relationship of *meaning* between 'star' and 'rats'. That suggests some other relationship. You can apply your 'word construction' checklist as in the previous category. In this case, a cursory check of the first and last letters, and their order, will reveal the simple, back-to-front relationship. It remains then to test each word with the precise relationship you have discovered. Thus 'star' is the reverse of 'rats', or 'star' is 'rats' read backwards. By replacing 'is to' with words that make more specific sense of the relationship, it becomes easy. 'Ward' is 'the reverse of ... 'or 'ward' is 'read backwards'. Sometimes you can get into a twist working out exact relationships (like in the sock and gloves example) when a simple technique like this can save you the bother.

Improving your chances

Some tests have multiple answer questions. These sometimes include a 'don't know' option. By never choosing 'don't know', you will increase your score chances and give yourself a one-in-five or one-in-six chance (depending on the number of answer choices) just by guessing.

Here is an example:

Eye is to **light** as **ear** is to:

- ☐ hearing
- ☐ sound
- ☐ nose
- ☐ music
- ☐ don't know

This tip applies to any multiple answer questions in a test.

Solution: sound.

Find the word that fits

Find the word from the bottom list that fits the top list:

division marine contract tenant

addition agreement country title storm

Solution: title. (It can be prefixed by 'sub' to make another word.)

This is a popular type of IQ question that requires a slightly different approach to those we have met so far. As with previous questions, before looking at the words in the lower list, you need to know what relates them to the words in the top list. What common feature do they share?

In this case each word forms another common word by the addition of a certain prefix. A glance at the lower list will soon reveal the answer, which forms the word 'subtitle'. Once again, it is quickly obvious that the words have no common meaning (such as animals, or girl's names). So, as in the earlier questions, you need to find some other common feature. This may be to do with the structure or letter content of the actual words (use your checklist), or – in this case – a possible relationship with another word. You need to determine this before turning to the lower list. Without a reasonable guess at a relationship you will make no sense of the lower list, however long you try. Having said that, you may not be sure about, in this case, whether there is such a word as 'subcontract'. Hardly likely in this example, but in more difficult questions there may well be at least one word you are not certain about. As we saw earlier, you only need to test two or three words to identify your common feature. Moreover (more good news), the lower list will probably include a *well-known* example of the common feature – in this case 'subtitle' – rather than an obscure example. In other words, the word that fits, once you find it, fits *easily*. This is often a good final test of whether you have got the correct answer.

The real job, then, is to spot the common feature. Having done that, you have cracked it. So keep your thinking logical, and follow these methods as a matter of routine.

As in earlier types of question, don't be satisfied with the first, feasible word fit. In this case you may have been attracted to 'subagreement', which doesn't sound too bad, but 'subtitle' is a more likely fit. Although this requires fast testing of possible connections, it may in the end boil down to your familiarity with words and their meanings. In short, it is far from culture-free, and this is another example of the value of test-taking skills.

Here's another of this type:

Find the word in the second line which will fit best into the first line:

ship	speed	man	terminal	space
healthy	insured	sick	well	tired

Solution: sick. (It can be prefixed by 'air' – to make another word.)

This time a less common prefix, 'air' – not a common, 'general purpose' prefix like 'sub' – fits the bill. Nonetheless, once you spot the kind of (prefix/suffix) question it is, the search can be simple.

Take any word on the first line and try it out for a prefix or suffix word that will create a common meaning. Then test it on the next word, then the next. As with earlier examples, if you can't find a common fit on two or maybe three words, don't spend more time. If your guess doesn't check out on two or more words it certainly will not apply to them all.

Had you checked for suffixes first, rather than prefixes, you might have tried 'shipwreck', 'shipshape', or 'shipmate'. Testing on the next word only, 'speed', quickly eliminates those suffix variants ('speedwreck', 'speedshape', etc). Checking then for prefix words, and using the same process, you might consider 'midship', 'flagship', 'kinship', or 'worship'.

It may help to say the word aloud: '...ship'. Hear what 'comes to mind'. Using your senses more fully is simply better 'thinking' (ie smarter). In any case you may work out your own system as you practise. A common method, for instance, is to work through the alphabet. Thus, 'a. ... ship', 'b ... ship' and so on. Usually this provides enough of a clue for your brain to throw up common word connections. The prefix 'air' would probably have been spotted immediately using this ABC technique, but don't expect them all to come so early in the alphabet.

Just for practice:

Find the word in the second line which will fit best into the first line:

lady	lord	mark	slide	mass

locked	tested	opened	closed

Solution: locked. (It can be prefixed by 'land'.)

Prefixes and suffixes

In many cases the missing word will be a prefix or suffix, and fortunately a relatively short list of these account for most of the connected words.

For example:

Back: -fire, -gammon, -ground, -hand, -lash, -log
Under: -ground, -study, -bid, -cover, -dog, -carriage
Over: -pass, -seas, -hear, -lap, -rule, -night, -hang, -run

You will notice that some of the new words use common suffixes, such as:

-ground (foreground, playground, underground, fairground)
-hand (forehand, offhand, underhand).

More common prefixes include: con-, com-, inter-, re-, ante-, post-. This is another example of where a simple checklist will account for a large percentage of questions in this category, and render tricky questions routine.

This takes care of a large proportion of the 'find the word that fits' questions you are likely to meet. But keep your mind open for exceptions to the rule. 'Worship', for instance, is not a common example of the '-ship' suffix.

Find the missing word

This next type of question is popular, and you have probably met it in newspaper and magazine puzzle sections.

Insert the word missing from the brackets:

policeman	(Mars)	nurse
solicitor	(________)	barrister

The first task is to find a relationship between both words on the upper line, and the bracketed word in the middle. You will again have to open your mind to relationships other than the meaning of the words. As we have already seen, the letters often hold the key. In this case a quick scan shows that the letters in the middle word appear in the outer words. The first two, 'ma' in the first word and the second two, 'rs', in the second word. You will then notice that in both cases, these are the last but one and last but two letters. Applying that relationship to the lower line is then straightforward.

Solution: The answer is 'tote'.

A 'real word' confirms your correct solution.

The following question is a variation on the theme.

worker	(roam)	amaze
tester	(______)	omen

Once again, the letters in brackets appear in the adjacent words, and once again their position has a common feature. In this case, the first two ('ro') and last two ('am') bracketed letters are the third and second letters from the respective adjacent words, appearing in that order. Your job is just about done at this point as the solution 'seem' fits the pattern.

Asymmetry

Here is another variation:

grid	(ring)	hang
stir	(______)	gaff

This is the same idea but the letters don't relate to the words *symmetrically*. Instead, they are second and third, and third and fourth respectively. Having had practice on the earlier ones, the missing word 'tiff' should have come easily. You will now be ready for just about anything of this particular type.

For example:

house	(head)	aged
bride	(_______)	lint

Easy? The missing word is 'belt'. As you have found, you don't need to be super-intelligent. You just need to know. And you get to *know* by *learning* – which anyone can do. This is a good example of a principle which applies to all questions of this type. It couldn't have less to do with hereditary intelligence. Just don't get too confident – there are exceptions to every rule.

Just for practice

The following are just for practice, if you wish.

ardour	(rain)	ninety
oppression	(_______)	trappings

Solution: port. (The second and first letters of each word, in that order.)

simpleton	(test)	stetson
quarry	(_______)	winning

Solution: rain. (Third and fourth letters from the end.)

However, notice in this case there are more choices. You need to check out each alternative. The final test, of course, is that you finish up with a real word. If you find more than one, choose the most common. Introducing alternative possible answers like this is about as close as an IQ question ever gets to being sneaky, which is a consoling thought for serious test-takers like us.

Knowing your ABCs

This category of question is as easy as ABC.

Which letter logically fills the gap?

A B C D ? F

Solution: E. No prizes so far.

Once again, find the missing letter:

A D G J ?

Solution: M. Still no more than ABCs, but this time missing two letters between the letters in the row.

Just like the previous types, 'alphabetical series' is a specific kind of verbal test, which you will soon get the hang of. By graduating gently as you learn how the principle can be applied, you need not be floored when you meet a tricky example. By doing your homework, you can count on easy scores from this type of question. Unlike the earlier word questions, you don't need to know much more than your alphabet. The rest is test sophistication. Try another:

A B D G ? P

This time, the number of missing letters between the row of letters are 0, 1, 2, 3 and so on upwards. You may need to count on your fingers and toes in these more advanced examples, but still no IQ genes are called upon. Far better, however, to set yourself up with a simple grid of letters to numbers, and use this as you used the 'word construction' checklist earlier. This will earn its keep many times over, and it may even be worth memorizing it. The main thing is to take the easiest route to a solution – that's where intelligence comes in. Just write down the alphabet and number each letter as follows:

A B C D E F G H I J K L M N 0 P Q R S T U V W X Y Z

1 2 3 4 5 6 7 8 9 10 11 12 13 14 15 16 17 18 19 20 21 22 23 24 25 26

By transposing the series of letters into numbers, the question is changed from a tricky letter series to a simple number series. Using the grid, you will find that the known letters are numbered:

A	B	D	G	?	P
1	2	4	7	?	16

This becomes a simple number series, the numbers rising by 1, 2, 3 and so on. The missing letter is 11, equivalent, on your patent grid to K. You will meet examples of number series later.

What is the next letter in this sequence?

O T F S N E T F S N T T ?

Solution: T. (The first letters of odd numbers.)

Where letters bear no relationship to their position in the alphabet – forwards or backwards – it is a sure sign that you have met a variation on the ABC theme. When in new territory, you will have to think more laterally. But even in this case, a checklist of common variants will usually cover the cases you are likely to meet.

The letter/number mix we have just met is a common ABC question, so it's as well to start there. Reference to your grid will soon disappoint you if you hoped for a neat relationship. Think, however, about different ways that a letter can relate to a word. The letters might stand for the first letter of each number/word – 'ottf' standing for 1, 2, 3, 4, and so on. A couple of sips of coffee and the slightest alphabetic twist and you have 1, 3, 5, 7, 9 ('otfsn' etc) – that's right, odd numbers. It's still as easy as ABC, but easy in a different way.

Now you are in the magic circle, no prizes for solving the following series:

T F S E T T F S E T ?

Solution: T. (The first letters of even numbers, starting with 2.)

Having met these examples, you can add 'odd and even' to your ABC question checklist (and, by extension, prime numbers and other number characteristics if you are into that sort of thing, which, sadly, some test compilers are).

When each set of symbols change clothes in this way, the clue is the *random* appearance of letters, which means that the *logical* series must be in the numbers.

Now look at the following, and spot the 'odd and even' number connection:

E E E N E N N N N N

Answer: E. (Last letter of odd number words.)

It gets boring. No prizes for:

O R X T N E N N N Y

Answer: O. (Last letter of even number words.)

You just need to see patterns like these repeated 'Ns' a couple of times and you will zoom into a solution in seconds, remembering these simple patterns.

The good news about very unusual relationships is that the stranger they are, the easier it is to remember them. It's just like a bizarre or extraordinary memory you can never forget. Thus an individual test question from years ago might be as memorable as a swotted-up checklist of common alternatives.

Here is another type of ABC question:

Fill in the appropriate letter at the question mark:

A B A C D C E F E G ? G I J I

Solution: H.

This is a good illustration of when to use your number/letter grid. Reading each letter off as a number, you get 121, 343, 565, 7?7, 9109. The missing number must be 8, equivalent to 'H'. This example is straightforward, but the letter/number grid would have made far more complex questions possible to crack.

'Letter squares' are another example of alphabet questions.

A	B	C	D	E
F	G	H	J	K
L	M	N	O	P
Q	R	S	T	U
V	W	X	Y	Z

Here are the questions:

1. Find the letter that comes between the letter between A and L and the letter between N and X. (M)
2. Find the letter that comes just before the letter just above the letter between M and O. (G)
3. Find the letter that comes just after the letter that comes just above the letter just before the letter just above N. (C)
4. Find the letter that comes just above the letter which comes just after the letter which comes between the letter just above N and the letter just below L. (H)
5. Find the letter that comes just below the letter which comes between the letter just after the letter just above F and the letter just before the letter just below K. (N)

These questions can be confusing unless you adopt a strategy. Take question 4 as an illustration. Starting from the end of the description and working towards the beginning, divide the question into five components – the relative positions of the letters.

Then find the letters, step by step:

Find the letter 5 that comes just above 4, the letter that comes just after 3, the letter that comes between 2, the letter just above N, 1, and the letter just below L. 1, the letter just below L = Q: Now continue: 2 = H, 3 = M, 4 = N, 5 = H.

Identification

Insert the letter W above or below the line.

B	C	D	E	J	K	N	P
	A	H	M	T	U	V	

You don't need language skills to answer this type of problem. In fact it can be misleading when it comes alongside the earlier questions.

Solution: Below the line. (The location depends on a physical characteristic. All letters below the line are symmetrical about a vertical axis.)

A little bit sneaky, but once you eliminate an alphabetic series, and the sort of relationships we met earlier, you are just left with letter *shapes*. Once you think in terms of shapes, or physical characteristics. you are close to cracking it.

Following the same principle, another question would be:

Insert the letters S and R above or below the line:

K	L	M	N	O
J	B	D	P	

Solution: S above, R below the line. (The shape of the letters above the line consist of either straight lines or curves, while the shape of those letters below is a mixture of straight lines and curves.)

Having tackled a few questions like this, it is soon apparent that there is a limit to the number of questions that can be asked. So, more than likely, you will be looking for curves and straight lines, above and below the line in the case of lower case letters, symmetry/asymmetry. Having met a few versions, you will see that it's another case for a checklist (straight/curved, symmetrical/asymmetrical about the vertical, symmetrical/asymmetrical about the horizontal, etc). Any new variation you meet is added to your checklist.

Flawed test questions

So far these tests have called on your problem-solving ability, or intelligence. However, many verbal tests assume some specialized knowledge or a bigger vocabulary. These are not proper IQ tests as they offend against the basic principle which should govern all such tests, even with their known limitations. It's as well to become familiar with these types of question, as a key principle is not to be surprised. On meeting such a question, at worst you can skip it and only return to it if you have time. Some examples of flawed test questions follow in the next paragraphs.

Which of the following cities is not located in Europe?

London Budapest Munich Tangier Geneva Graz

You might find this easy and pick out the correct city. Even so, it is nonsensical to include it in an IQ test. You either know that Tangier is in Africa or you don't. At any rate, it has nothing to do with your intelligence. The question would probably be posed along 'odd one out' lines, but the objection still applies.

Even more obscure are questions making a demand on your vocabulary beyond basic English. A member of MENSA devised this test for the supposedly 'super-intelligent':

Which does not belong?

dada abstract expressionist cubist dodecaphonic pointillist

Don't give it another thought. This is a problem which belongs in an examination for second-year art students, not in an IQ test. It betrays a lack of understanding on the part of the deviser of the difference between an intelligent person and an academic who has enjoyed specialized education.

Even more extreme would be the following analogy taken from a book dealing with intelligence tests, under the heading 'Match Wits with MENSA':

Roquefort is to France as Liederkranz is to ...

Solution: USA. (Liederkranz is an American cheese named after a singing group organized by a cheese producer of German origin. Armed with that piece of [peripheral] knowledge, any test subject would make light work of the question; without it, the question is unanswerable, however intelligent the subject.)

Top-scoring tips

The 'verbal skills' you have learnt so far are mainly test techniques. You are simply preparing for the different kinds of questions you will meet, and developing a strategy to tackle them in as routine a fashion as possible. That might require a bit of memorizing, such as a checklist or a letter/number grid, and some practice. But the process does not require special intelligence and nor does using the techniques increase your verbal intelligence materially, just your test sophistication score.

However, there are ways to increase your actual verbal intelligence generally. Thus you can boost your IQ score beyond the several points you can gain by test sophistication and familiarity. We can all apply these intelligence-increasing strategies. Nor is there any shortage of books and training courses. It is fairly conventional, common-sense learning. Here are some tips, and there are no shortcuts:

- Read, read, and read. Read different sorts of books from those you have read in the past. Try reading three times as fast and don't worry about what you remember. Read a favourite classical novel again, slowly, savouring every line and making a note of things you had not noticed before;
- Make friends with a good dictionary that gives word roots and synonyms. Not only are word derivations often fascinating, but also they add immeasurably to your understanding and enjoyment of prose, and enrich your day-to-day vocabulary;
- Stay intellectually fresh by helping your children with their homework;
- Start to take an interest in new hobbies, sports, pastimes and people. Don't let your mind vegetate;
- If you have to tackle a psychometric test, review this chapter and practise some of the methods;
- Study logic and linguistics;
- Learn a foreign language;
- Try your hand at writing articles or books, or journalism.

Remember, verbal reasoning is just one aspect of intelligence. It is one of many areas of intelligence in which you can improve and excel if you decide to.

Numerical skills: tests to try yourself

The second main category of IQ question is numerical. It embodies similar principles to some of the verbal tests, but questions are dressed in arithmetical garb.

Number series

A numerical series is a sequence of numbers which follows a specific, identifiable pattern. The simplest example is:

1 2 3 4 5 6 7 8 9 ?

Solution: 10.

Now, what about:

1 3 2 4 3 5 4 6 5 7 ?

Solution: 6.

A useful first step, which is a key to many numerical tests, is to write down the differences between all adjacent numbers, thus:

1 [+2] 3 [–1] 2 [+2] 4 [–1] 3 [+2] 5 [–1] 4 [+2] 6 [–1] 5 [+2] 7 [–1]?

In this way you will neatly arrive at the pattern. In this case, two is added, one taken off, and the process repeated.

There are other ways of considering a number series. Using the same example, you will see that it consists of two interlinked series:

1 2 3 4 5 ?

3 4 5 6 7 ?

You will meet this sort of question in many different forms. Try:

2 3 4 6 6 9 8 12 10 15 12 ?

Here, differences alone will make no sense, but two inter-linked series will.

Solution: 18. (The two series are 2, 4, 6, 8, 10, 12 and 3, 6, 9, 12, 15.)

Here is another example:

1	3	7	15	?
240	48	12	4	?

Solution:

31
2

In the top row add 2, 4, 8, 16. In the bottom row start on the right, and, beginning with 2, multiply consecutive numbers by 2, 3, 4 and 5.

Improving your chances

You will sometimes get multiple answer questions. As with verbal reasoning questions, a 'don't know' option offers you a chance of free points. Never answer 'don't know'. A guess will give you at least a percentage chance of getting the right answer.

Here is an example:

1 2 4 7 ? 16

- ☐ 11
- ☐ 13
- ☐ 10
- ☐ 12
- ☐ Don't know

Solution: 11

Analogies

As with verbal questions, you will meet analogies in the numerical part of a test.

Select the correct answer from the line below:

⅓ is to 3, as 3 is to ?

6 ⅙ 9 12 27

Solution: 27. (3 is 9 times ⅓, and 27 is 9 times 3.)

In the following example no alternative answers are given.

If ⅔ is 4, how much is 3?

Do this the right way around – if ⅔ is 4, 3 is ? In fractions it can be stated like this:

If ⅔ is $^{12}/_{3}$, $^{9}/_{3}$ is ?

Solution: 18. (The answer must be 6 times as much, namely $^{54}/_{3}$ or 18.)

Or you may prefer to use an equation. For example:

If ⅞ is 1¾, how much is 1½ ?

In arithmetic terms, this would be:

$\frac{7}{8} : 1\frac{3}{4} = 1\frac{1}{2} : x$

As an equation, this would be:
$\frac{7}{8}x = 1\frac{3}{4}$ times $1\frac{1}{2}$

Turn it into fractions and simplify:
$$\frac{7x}{8} = \frac{168}{64} = \frac{21}{8}$$

Therefore, $x = 3$

If you enjoy arithmetic, these will present no problem. In any event, by doing a basic maths course you will soon acquire the 'hereditary intelligence' these tests are designed to measure. The important thing is that you can do something about your IQ, just by learning basic arithmetic. If you choose not to, you are no less intelligent. Suffice to say that you can be more intelligent in the ways you want to be. Life is too short to spend on things you don't enjoy or conform to somebody else's opinion as to what is important.

Finish it off

Have a go at this one:

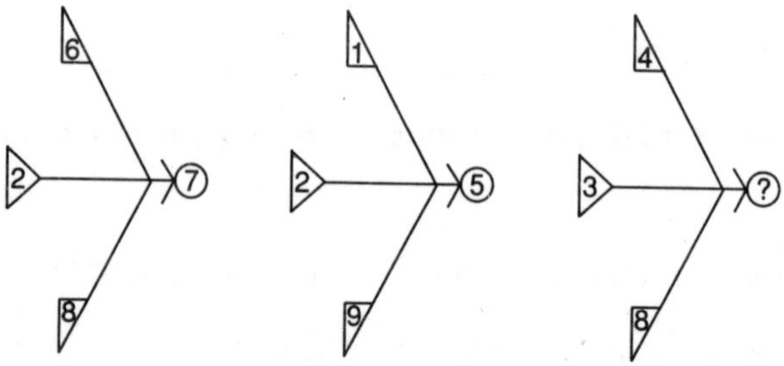

These types of completion, or 'finish it off' tests are trial-and-error exercises using arithmetic operations such as divisions, multiplications, subtractions and additions in various combinations. Squares are rarely used (hooray!). There will often be a shortcut to the solution.

In the above example, 7 cannot be a product (2 × 6, 2 × 8, 8 × 6). Neither can it be a sum (2 + 6, 8 + 6, 2 + 8) or a fraction of even numbers. That leaves division. In this case, 'add the wings and divide by the tail' is the correct fit, so the solution is 4.

The next question follows the same principle. Note that different geometrical figures usually indicate different arithmetic operations.

Insert the missing number:

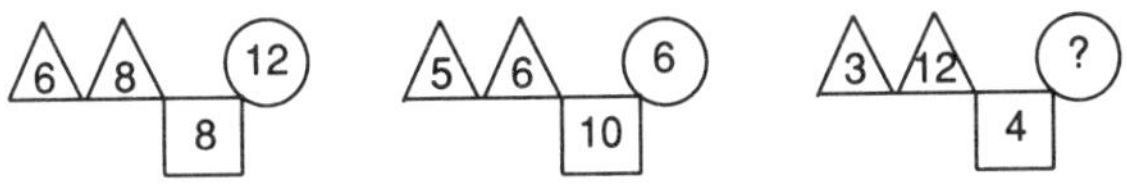

Solution: 18. (Multiply the triangles and divide by half of the square.)

This one doesn't really fit into a neat pattern, so a bit of trial-and-error is needed. However, the presence of an odd number in the third series of numbers suggests that multiplication is necessary at some point in the calculation. Try multiplying the triangles: the answers are all even numbers and are all larger than the circle. Therefore, to obtain the circle, there must then be a division. Dividing by the number in the square gives half the result, so divide by half the number in the square and you will arrive at your solution.

The danger with all complex, trial-and-error exercises is that you get flustered and start going in circles. They can be as much of a psychological as an intellectual challenge, especially if a test is supervised or you are under pressure, such as in an examination-type situation. Although it is easier said than done, relaxation is the answer. Deliberate deep breathing will help, however stressed you are. When in a relaxed, carefree frame of mind, even if you can't tackle a question, you are less likely to freeze up and waste time unnecessarily. Move on to the next question. You can probably complete two or three more questions in the time you take to ponder a tricky one. If you have time to spare, go back to the question you missed. If you don't, at least you have used your time to best effect.

Some tests in the numerical section can be verbal in disguise, like the ones you did earlier. For example:

1586	(1631)	3521
8432	(______)	5289

Solution: 8259. (First and last numbers go consecutively in the brackets).

That should not have been too difficult. However, some tests along these lines can be more difficult, involving arithmetical operations. For example, look at:

2569	(1183)	1386
7242	(______)	5321

Solution: 1921. (Deduct the right side from the left side.)

In another variant, instead of adding or deducting numbers, add or subtract the sum of the digits on each side:

1234	(36)	5678
2345	(____)	6789

Solution: 44. (Add all the digits together.)

As you can see, there are only so many variations to the theme. With an open mind, and a mental checklist based on the sorts of questions you have met, common questions of this type become routine.

Number squares

Number squares will invariably involve arithmetical operations. These are mainly additions and subtractions, less frequently divisions and multiplications, and a combination of two operations is often used. Solving these completion problems is largely based on trial-and-error, so the best route towards a technique is by several examples.

6	17	11
5	14	9
?	11	8

Solution: 3. (Deduct the left digit from the middle number to give the right digit.)

Here is a more difficult problem:

2	6	3	4
2	8	4	4
3	5	?	5

Solution: 3. (Multiply the figures in the first two columns, and divide the product by the digit in the third column to give the number in the fourth column.)

Number wheels

Another form of 'finish it off' question is 'number wheels':

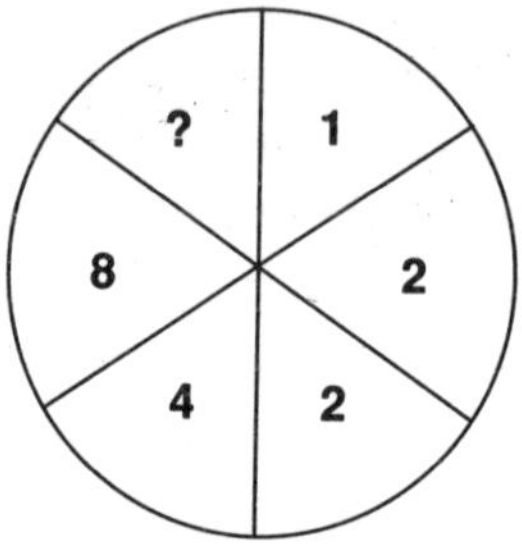

These are also trial-and-error exercises, but you can still apply a sort of system. First try sums of opposites. Or work your way around the wheel looking at ascending or descending differences and products. If none of these yields a result, try adding or subtracting the same number or going up or down.

Solution: 32 (Working clockwise, 1 × 2 = 2, 2 × 2 = 4, 2 × 4 = 8, 4 × 8 = 32.)

Here's another number wheel:

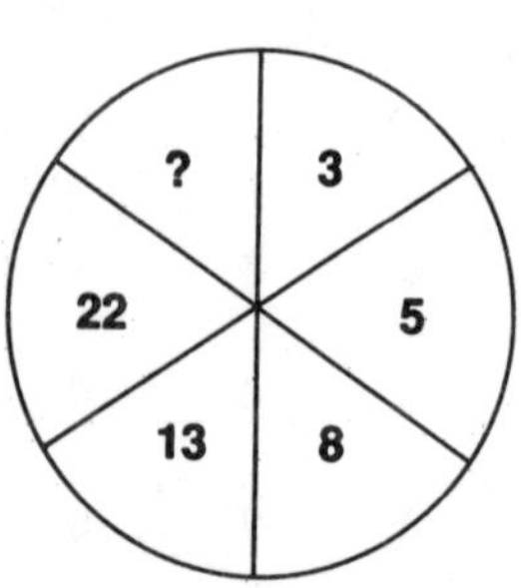

Solution: 39. (Working clockwise, multiplying the number in the segment by 2, then deducting, successively, 1, 2, 3, etc.

$2 \times 3 - 1 = 5$, $2 \times 5 - 2 = 8$, $2 \times 8 - 3 = 13$, $2 \times 13 - 4 = 22$, $2 \times 22 - 5 = 39$.)

Here's a slightly more difficult one:

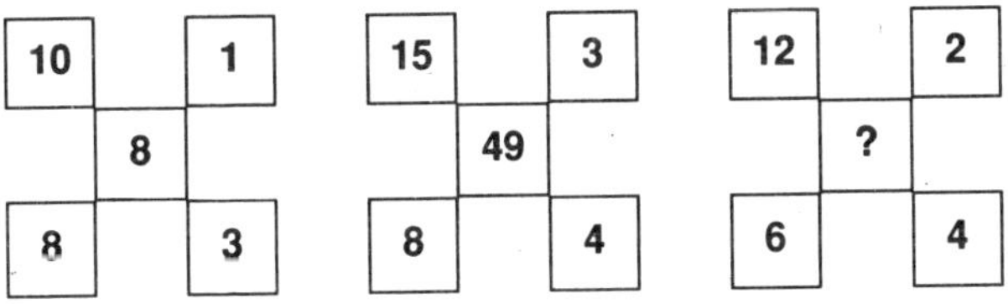

Study it carefully with a view to finding a short cut. The first of the three figures offers no ready clue, but look at the second. No additions and no subtractions will result in 49. Division is equally unlikely as the lowest would be 98 divided by 2, and there is no way to arrive at 2. So look at multiplication: 49 is 7×7 (thank goodness for multiplication tables and parrot-fashion learning). Seven is the sum of the right squares and the difference between the left squares. You're there.

Solution: 36 (4 + 2 from the right column = 6, multiplied by the difference between the figures in the left column = 6).

Top-scoring tips

Numerical IQ questions follow the same sort of principles as verbal reasoning when it comes to test sophistication.

- There are several types of question that continually recur in different garb.
- There are no trick questions. At worst, a question is designed to hide the sort of question it is (which then makes it easier).

- Unlike verbal tests, you don't need to exercise your vocabulary and understanding of the nuances of language.
- You don't need special arithmetic skills – like high-speed addition and mental long division. The questions test logic, reasoning and relationships rather than raw numerical dexterity.
- Just as reading will help your verbal skills, you can improve your numerical intelligence by undertaking any sort of maths training, such as a DIY 'teach yourself' book, or a GCSE qualification. In short, by improving your numerical education.

Visual–spatial

The third main category of IQ questions is visual–spatial (or visio–spatial). These questions cover the same sort of logical skills as the first two types, except that you are now dealing in shapes and graphical relationships. Some people are more at home with these, and that just reflects our different thinking styles – spatial skills are associated with the right-side of the brain, whereas the symbols and language required for the first two types of test are more associated with the left-side of the brain. But neither type of question demands skills you can't learn. Once you get a bit of know-how and practice under your belt, you may well start to enjoy doing tests that you previously steered clear of. The more familiar you are with the type of question (forget about 'fixed' intelligence), the more you are likely to do well and enjoy the process into the bargain.

Have a go at visual–spatial tests

Choose one figure from the six numbered figures that belongs logically in the empty square.

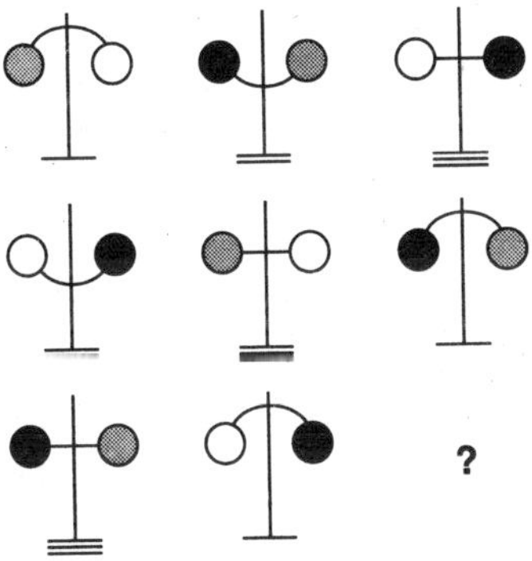

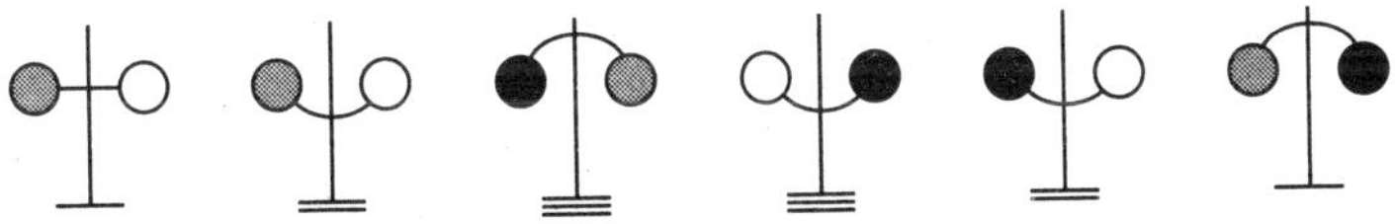

1 2 3 4 5 6

Do this systematically. It is worth getting the basics right as you can depend on getting this kind of question. Notice first what each figure consists of – the variables:

1. The base has one, two or three horizontal lines.
2. The crossbar is straight, bent upwards or bent downwards.
3. The circles are black + white, black + shaded or white + shaded.

Now all you have to do is find which features are missing in the bottom row and right column. First, notice that the two-line base is missing, so the answer is either 2 or 5. Then notice that the white + shaded circles are needed, which identifies number 2 as the correct figure. In this case the crossbar is not even needed for identification, although number 2 fits the bill anyway. Easy.

Now try another, using the same procedure:

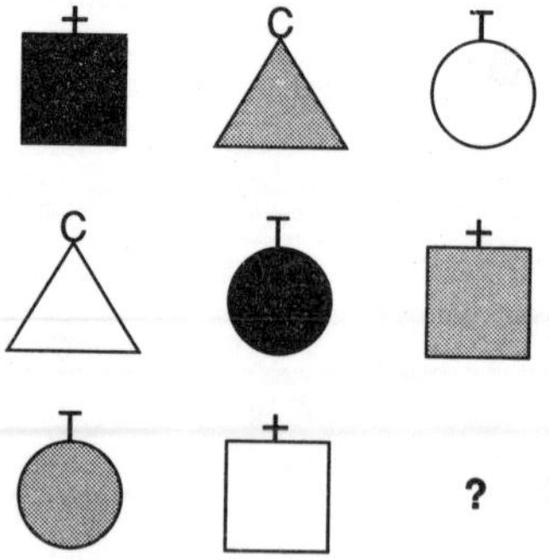

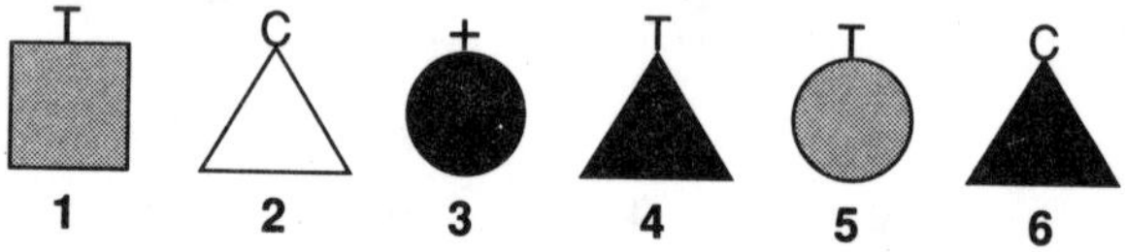

Solution: 6. (A triangle is missing, so the answer is either 2, 4 or 6. A 'C' is missing, eliminating 4. The black triangle is needed, identifying number 6 as the solution.)

Here is another test for you to solve using the same technique:

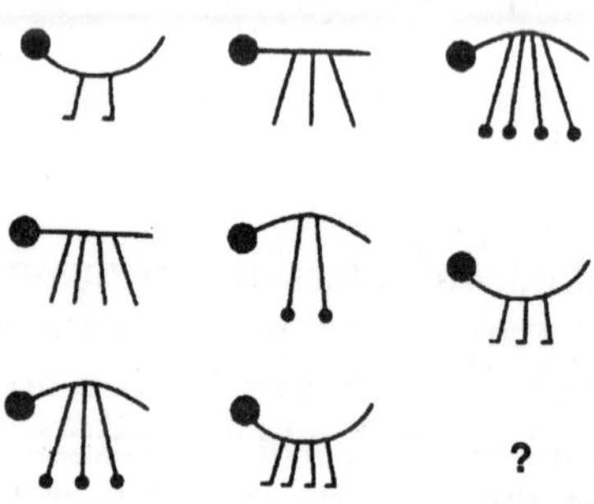

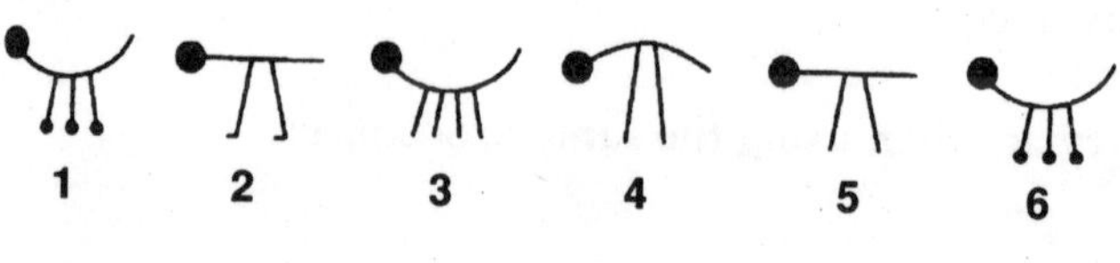

Solution: 5. (Using the same steps as before, a straight body is missing, so 2 and 5 would qualify. However, legs without shoes are missing, leaving 5. A double check by counting the number of legs leaves you in no doubt.)

Some selection tests are more complex. For example, identify the correct figure from the six numbered ones to replace the question mark.

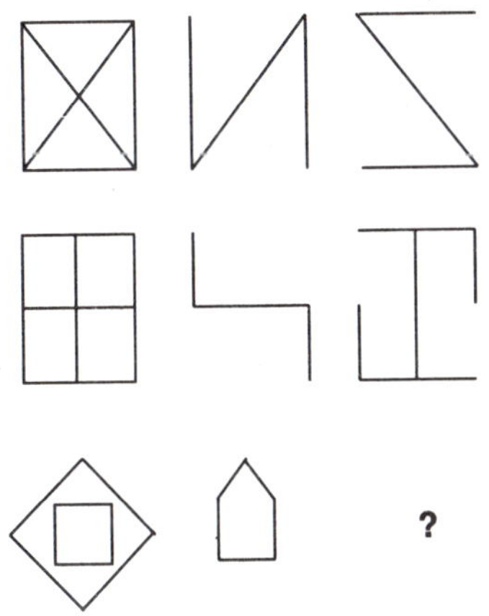

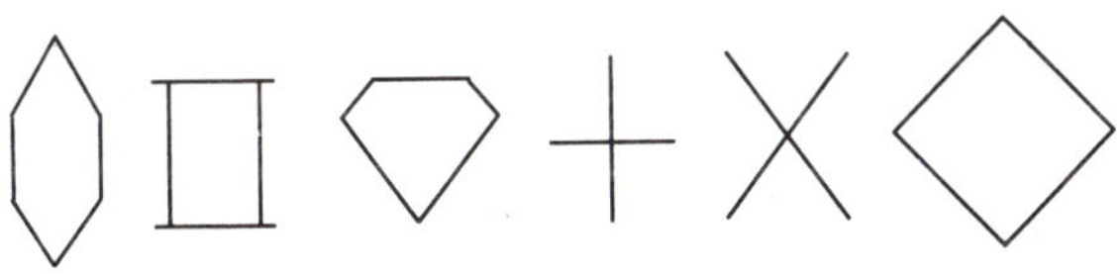

1 2 3 4 5 6

Solution: 3. (This follows a different principle from previous 'selection' type questions. The lines of the drawings in the second column are taken away from the first column to leave the third column. In other words, super-imposing the second and third columns gives the figure in the first column.)

A third type of selection test follows an entirely different line. Which belongs in the empty space?

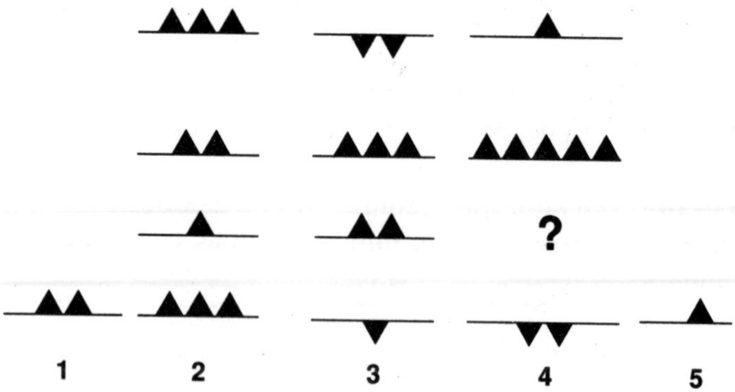

Solution: 2. (Each triangle over the line counts as +1, and each below -1.)

There is no standard way to recognize visual–spatial tests like these, which are arithmetical in disguise. The symbols differ in numbers rather than in design, and are placed in two distinct locations, either above or below a line (as in this case) or inside/outside a geometrical figure.

The following alternative uses different symbols (male and female) instead of locations.

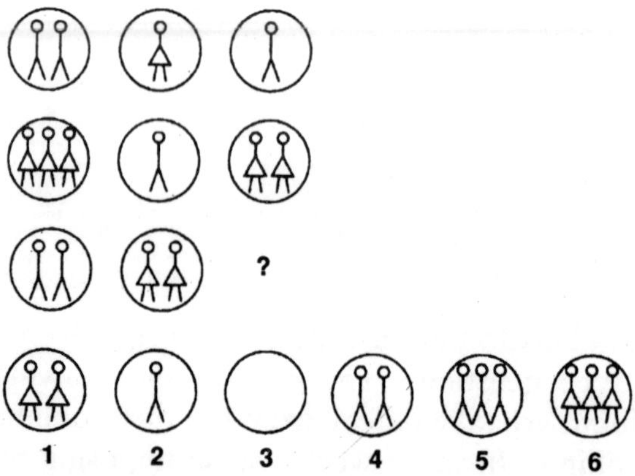

Solution: 3. (Men + 1, women – 1; 2 – 2 = 0. The right hand column is the product of the first two.)

Here is another example, this time with different symbols instead of locations to denote plus and minus:

(O O O) (□□) (O)

(O O) (□□□) (□)

(□□□) (O O O) (?)

(□□) (O O O) ( ) (□) (O)

1 2 3 4 5

Solution: 3. (Circles are plus, squares are minus. The right hand column is the product of the first two.)

By now you will have gained enough experience to deal with most visio-spatial selection tests. There are, however, some that contain a twist likely to baffle you unless you are well prepared. Here are two such examples.

Select the figure in the second row which would logically replace the question mark.

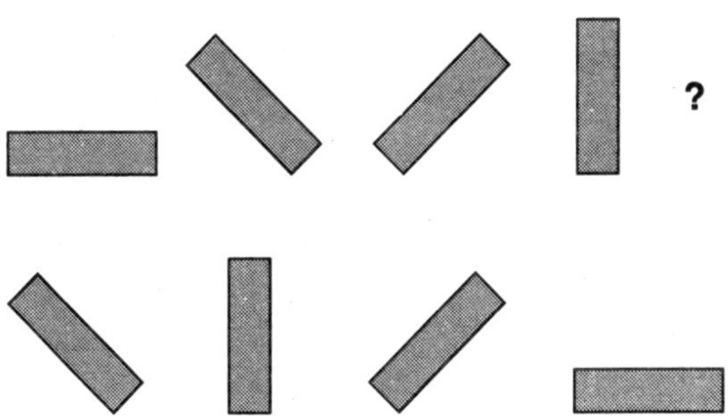

1 2 3 4

Solution: 2. (The rectangle turns clockwise with an increment of 45° each time, ie 45°, 90°, 135° and 180°.)

Select the figure in the second row, which would logically replace the question mark.

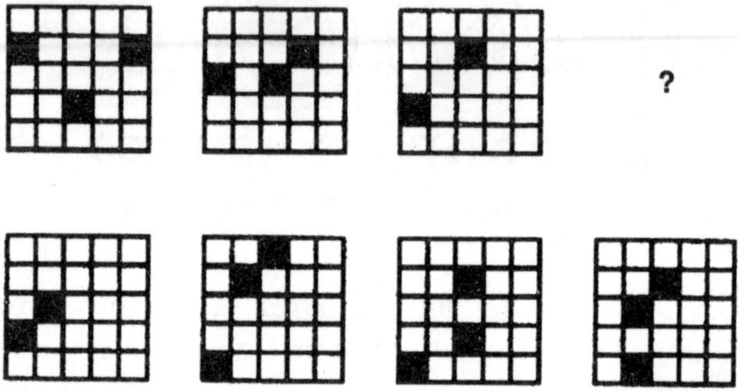

1 2 3 4

Solution: 2. (The black square in the first column moves one square down each time, in the third column one square up, and in the fifth column one square to the left. The fact that two black squares fuse into one in the third form left figure can be confusing.)

All these visio-spatial examples are perfectly legitimate in their variety. However, there are some authors who specialize and excel in devising tests which are as difficult to break as a wartime code. Don't worry about them, they are not appropriate for a valid IQ test. Just for fun, though, here is an example:

Find the appropriate numbered figure to fill the empty space in the top row.

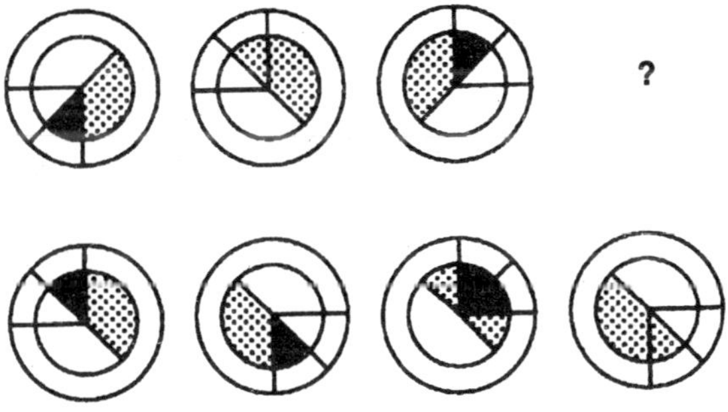

1 2 3 4

Solution: 4. (The two conjoined sectors of the outer circle rotate clockwise, and the dotted sector of the inner ring, rotates counter-clockwise. Whenever the black sector is outside the dotted sector, it disappears. Forget it! It is easier to construct obscure tests than to solve them.)

Odd one out?

Which is the odd one out?

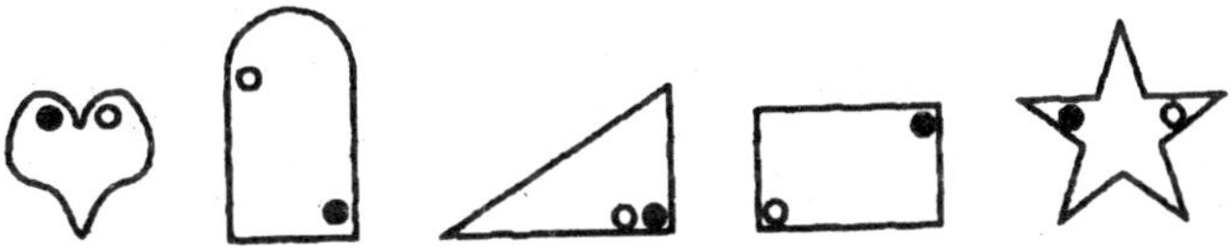

1 2 3 4 5

Solution: 3. (Each can be divided symmetrically, with a dot in each half, except 3.)

Symmetry crops up quite a lot in spatial tests, so it's worth adding it to your mental checklist.

In the following example you have to find the three odd ones out (ignore the arrow for the moment):

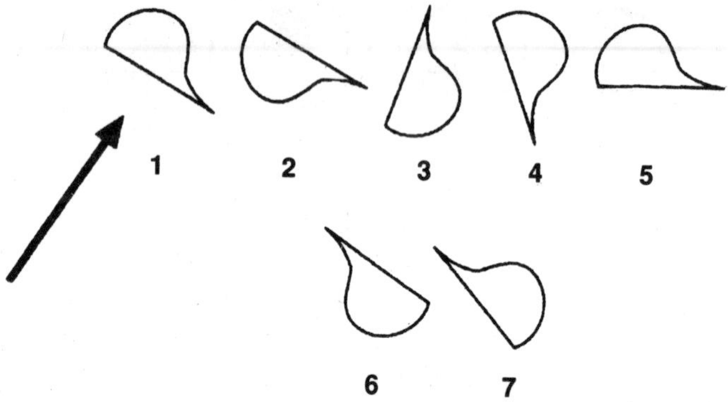

These can sometimes be confusing and time-consuming. You will probably turn the figures around in your mind's eye to see which are congruent and which are not, and quite possibly you will try several times. As was said earlier, some people can do this sort of spatial test more easily than others, as it is a characteristic of brain hemisphere preference. There is, however, a very simple method, which will provide a solution.

Look at the base and just establish whether, viewed from the straight line as indicated by the arrow, the peak points right or left. Numbers 2, 3 and 7 point to the left.

Solution: 2, 3 and 7.

It might help to jot down left (L) and right (R) as you proceed from 1 to 7 so that you don't forget where you are:

1	2	3	4	5	6	7
R	L	L	R	R	R	L

The same principle applies to all tests of this type, so a couple more examples should be enough.

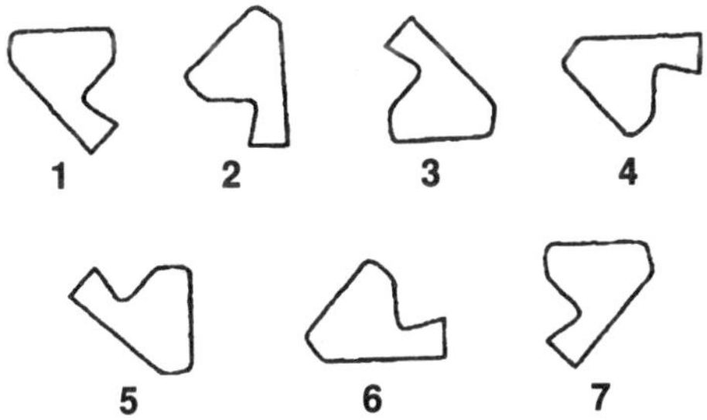

Solution: 1, 3 and 6. (The other four can be rotated into each other.)

Analogies

Analogies turn up everywhere, including in visual–spatial tests. Try this one.

Find the figure that completes the analogy:

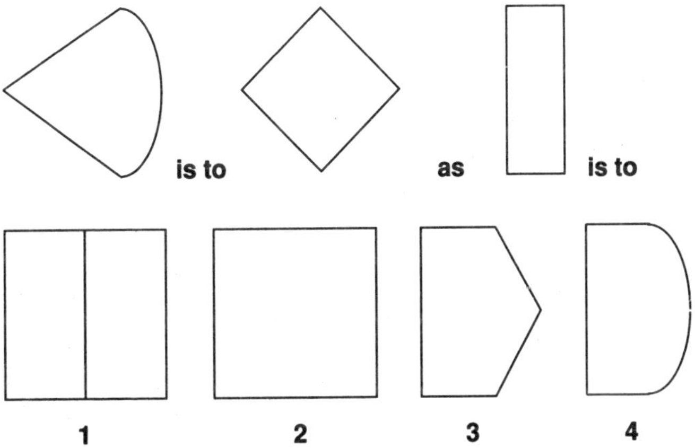

Solution: 2 (Remove the right-hand edge, and replace it with a mirror image of the remainder).

Top scoring tips

Visual–spatial tests are not as culturally contaminated as either verbal or numerical tests, which require language and maths knowledge respectively. Some of the top scoring tips in the previous two question categories will apply equally to the visual–spatial part of a test. But any conventional learning that will familiarize you with handling shapes, dimensions and perspectives will help. For instance, a basic geometry course will include symmetry and the characteristics of basic shapes.

Even visual–spatial tests – the ones said to be 'culture-free' – assume that 'innate intelligence' means writing things on paper, starting at top left and going in lines towards bottom right, using language to communicate the questions and incorporating Arabic numerals extensively. Such cultural know-how would not be of much survival value for a street child in Rio, let alone a person from outside urban culture.

The good news is that the test skills you have learnt for this part of the IQ test will significantly increase your score, as will straightforward practice, without major re-education. Some people really get to enjoy these tests that don't require vocabulary and maths skills, and do them as a hobby. Enjoyment will do wonders for your IQ score.

3

Knowing yourself: intrapersonal intelligence

Intrapersonal intelligence ('intra', meaning within, as against 'inter' meaning among) concerns knowing what you feel, and how to act wisely on that self-knowledge. People who score high on intrapersonal intelligence factors will be described as being 'in touch with their feelings'. They feel good about themselves. They are positive and content about what they are doing in life. Not only do they know how they feel, but they also know how to express those feelings. They know who they are as people. They are confident in themselves, their ideas and their ability to convey them to others. They know what they want and what is important to them.

This chapter covers three main aspects of intrapersonal intelligence:

- knowing yourself: five characteristics of intrapersonal intelligence;
- knowing what you want: the self-knowledge of personal goals and purposes;

- knowing what's important: the self-knowledge of personal values.

Knowing yourself

Intrapersonal intelligence involves knowing yourself in different ways:

- emotional self-awareness;
- assertiveness;
- self-esteem;
- independence;
- self-actualization.

Emotional self-awareness

This personal competency gives you the freedom to know yourself and the ability to share and express that awareness. It means you are not locked into yourself, in a sort of emotional prison. An inability to notice our true feelings leaves us at their mercy. People with greater certainty about their feelings are better pilots of their lives. They seem surer about personal decisions from whom to marry to what job to take. Emotional self-awareness is part of 'emotional literacy', and a sign of maturity and balance. It means being honest with yourself and others. Ask yourself:

- Are you able to recognize your feelings - how you truly feel?
- Can you differentiate between the different feelings you have?
- Do you know why you feel the way you do?

Self-awareness – recognizing a feeling as it happens – is the keystone of emotional intelligence. The ability to monitor feelings from moment to moment is crucial to psychological insight and self-understanding. This is a common emotional blind spot for many people. A person in mourning, for instance, may know only too well that he or she is sad, but fail to recognize that they are also angry with the person for dying – a feeling that seems inappropriate yet is harboured by the unconscious mind. In the same way, a parent who yells at their child who runs into the street looks and sounds angry, but their real emotion may be fear, and later perhaps, guilt.

People with no such self-awareness often 'blow up' emotionally when under pressure. They don't know what is happening to them, or how to handle their emotions. Such feelings don't go away. They may go underground, but will probably come to the surface some time later, unless they're dealt with.

Knowing and showing

Knowing your emotions does not mean expressing them. On the contrary, it is a cognitive ability that may well result in a choice *not* to express or act upon how you happen to feel, or to behave in a more appropriate way than your feelings would dictate. Aggression and 'letting off steam' are instinctive behaviours that don't require much neo-cortex type intelligence. Four-year-old children are pretty adept at expressing their emotions but not so good at being aware of them or controlling them. Such intelligence has to be nurtured, tested and developed in a world with other four- year-olds who have their own problems. Fortunately, we usually learn these social intelligences without being taught, although some people pick them up better than others.

Thinking and being

Personal characteristics of this sort require no special genetic endowment. Nor do they do demand self-knowledge skills such as meditation, acquired over many years. They are more about *thinking* and *being*, than *doing*. Usually, when we understand ourselves and manage our emotions, behaviour naturally follows. In other words, the doing takes care of itself. The important change happens inside. Behaviour will follow perception, or thinking, as surely as day follows night.

When it comes to improving this aspect of your intelligence, *awareness* is the lion's share of the task: awareness of the importance of self-knowledge; awareness of a whole inner world waiting to be discovered. This demands honesty rather than intellectual prowess. The first change will be in how you perceive yourself. The process is one of self-questioning and reflection, but it also requires an underlying commitment to live up to your full potential – what you want to do and be. Each aspect of human intelligence seems to be based on *purpose*.

It is possible to know who you are and how you feel, and to use that self-knowledge in a positive, intelligent way. Remember: you are the only one who knows your own mind. You are the only one in charge of your feelings. You generate them, and you are responsible for them. They are within your control – or can be. This is one aspect of intelligence that you can really do something about once you make the decision. In the process, you become more *intelligent* in a fuller meaning of the term. Simple guidelines will help you acquire important self-knowledge:

- give yourself time – make time;
- give yourself special attention and value – you are unique, and your interests paramount;
- reflect, muse, ponder, imagine;
- try to describe how you feel.
- recall positive, empowering, memories and notice how you now actually feel better.

You don't need special skills, and the process is both enjoyable and therapeutic. In any event, don't feel guilty about taking time out to get to know yourself better. The good news is that however immutable the world outside, you can always change inside, which is where worthwhile change has to start anyway.

Assertiveness

Assertiveness is sometimes confused with aggressiveness, especially in a competitive work environment. Aggressiveness is getting your way, no matter what (or who) gets in your way. Assertiveness is the emotional competency to freely and appropriately express your thoughts, feelings, opinions, and beliefs. Ask yourself these questions:

- Can you express your feelings, beliefs and thoughts to others, and defend them in a constructive way?
- Can you say 'No' without feeling guilty, when you know it is right to do so?
- Do you sometimes wish you had said what was on your mind in a meeting or group discussion rather than keeping silent, even though seething underneath?
- Do you tend to get your own way without making an issue of it?

With such 'emotional skills' you usually get what you want more effectively in the end. However, you can protect and foster relationships at the same time – relationships that may be important to you. Being honest and open about your feelings is not a sign of weakness. Nor should saying what you think in a courteous but constructive way be termed 'blunt' or 'domineering'. Both behaviours are characteristics of intra- and interpersonal intelligence. To speak when it would be easier to stay silent, not only do you need to have courage and emotional backbone, but be wise and smart into the bargain.

It is easy to get this one wrong. In the workplace, for instance, aggressiveness is sometimes fostered and interpreted as 'taking initiative'. Assertiveness, on the other hand, eliminates the belittling and disrespectful behaviours that are so often equated with initiative and success. Assertiveness is a sign of emotional integrity, and a mark of intelligence in a person. In an organizational culture of 'mutual assertiveness', employees will be more ready to speak up about how they feel, and express ideas they have. They are thus of more value to the organization.

Emotions such as aggression and anger more often than not lie below the surface. Sometimes outward agreement can mean disagreement and resentment underneath. People often don't say how they really feel. Sooner or later they suffer, along with customers, colleagues and the business itself. Emotional literacy of this sort is a high-value resource, and invaluable in personal and work relationships.

Assertiveness calls for a solid emotional foundation. You need to know your values and desires, be guided by them and be ready to act them out. Sometimes that means putting yourself in the firing line, and that takes courage. However, in many situations, assertiveness is a welcome liberator: 'Finally, someone spoke the truth.'

You can probably think of situations in which you should have been more assertive, and identify likely occasions in the future. If you feel this is an intelligence weak spot, there are books which address assertiveness in depth. For most of us, self-awareness – self-knowledge – is enough to make the difference. We get to know ourselves by honestly asking the above questions, and committing to the common sense changes we need to make in order to answer them to our satisfaction.

Self-esteem

Self-esteem, or self-image, is the emotional intelligence characteristic that shows a high self-worth and is an important source of self-confidence. It means you have feelings of adequacy – good feelings about who you are as a person. You feel satisfied with yourself. You are self-fulfilled. Ask yourself these questions:

- Do you respect and accept yourself, just as you are, 'warts and all'?
- Do you feel secure and self-confident most of the time?
- Would others who know you say you have a good 'sense of yourself', of 'who you are'?

You can always tell if an organization is low on self-regard among its employees. Morale is low; employees appear depressed; people are fearful and complaining; they have no pride in their work, products and company. The crux, of course, is self-image in individuals at every level. No technical skill or organizational status can make up for it.

An individual may not be able to affect a whole culture, of course. But we can all start to see ourselves in a more positive, optimistic light, and build on our strengths. Self-image – the way you see yourself – is a mental *resource* you can develop and change as you *choose*. You need never be stuck with it, however ingrained it may seem. What's in the mind has a habit of becoming reality. It affects our every behaviour and inevitably the behaviour of those around us. So self-esteem is not an optional intelligence extra. Even the most gifted person will achieve little if they undervalue themselves.

The late Maxwell Maltz wrote several landmark books about self-image, its ubiquitous effect on our lives, and how we can manage it. There's plenty you can do and resources you can draw upon if you recognize a need in this area. This author's book *The Right Brain Manager* covers self-image in more depth. For present purposes work on this presupposition:

For all practical purposes you are of infinite worth.

It takes true intelligence to recognize this and live up to our true potential.

Independence

Independence is a trait we associate with 'self-starters'. As a feature of emotional intelligence we can describe this 'label' more fully. 'Independent' people:

- are self-directed and self-controlled;
- have initiative;
- seem free, and not emotionally dependent;
- act with maturity, and people seem happy to follow and trust them,
- know how to take care of themselves;
- are self-reliant in planning;
- are able to make the important decisions for themselves;
- don't fall apart and wait for others to bail them out;
- enjoy relationships marked by mutual respect and responsibility;
- have integrity;
- are willing to take responsibility for their feelings, thoughts and actions;
- have their own inner standards;
- rely on others for help when necessary, but do not cling to other people to satisfy their emotional needs;
- don't live out of the 'psychological pocket' of other people.

This is not the stereotypical 140 IQ person, you will agree. Rather, a person displaying extraordinary emotional intelligence.

By taking responsibility for setting and living out your goals, you will foster this competence. By sorting out your own values and priorities, you will be less dependent on others. You will learn more about setting goals and identifying values later in the chapter.

Self-actualization

Probably no one on his or her deathbed ever said that they wished they had spent more time at the office. But all too many regret not having lived the life they felt they could and should have lived. Dr Carl Jung wrote that to come to the end of one's life and not to have lived one's mission is to have failed. Jung was very clear about the purpose of our lives: *individuation* or becoming alive as a full person. Ask yourself these questions:

- Are you realising your potential?
- Would you say you have a meaningful, rich and full life?
- Do you feel excited and satisfied with your accomplishments?

Self-actualization is how this is sometimes described. The term has appeared over the decades in popular psychology and self-help books, and is undoubtedly part of the emotional intelligence package. It means maximizing your potential. At the risk of sounding corny – which this emotional competence is certainly not – it means being *fulfilled.*

People with low EQ don't usually know what they want to do in life and don't care much about improving themselves. But it's never too late to find a new direction in your life and pursue real meaning. This will not correlate with intellectual, IQ-type intelligence. Self-actualization transcends rational thought, which can often be self-critical and limiting. Many intellectually gifted people fail to find purpose in their lives, until it is too late. Self-actualization is much nearer to true intelligence than raw intellect. For most people, finding meaning in life is a major, ongoing project. It relegates other concerns to second or less significant place.

Knowing what you want

Intelligent people tend to know what they want and where they are going in life. For that reason (among others) they tend to get what they want and arrive at where they are going to. They achieve. But this aspect of intelligence is not restricted to 'high fliers', 'goal-oriented', 'driven' people. We all have desires and goals.

This kind of intelligence can be augmented by goal-setting know-how. With such know-how you can increase your chances of success, and avoid pursuing goals you didn't really want, or wanted less than others you didn't get round to. In particular, intelligent goal setting involves your unconscious mind. Given direction, your unconscious mind will pilot your 'unthinking' behaviour (habits) to help you achieve what it understands that you want. With this sort of self-knowledge you can set your goals in such a way as to maximize the chance of their being fulfilled.

We are not always conscious of our desires and intentions. For instance, we might desire attention, respect, love, fame and so on without really being able to express it. Moment-to-moment we may not be aware of this. However, much of our behaviour will nonetheless be directed towards such unconscious, or unexpressed desires, as though an inner force is directing us. At the same time, these unconscious 'intentions' might work contrary to conscious goals. Pulling in two directions usually ends in failure. We don't achieve the conscious goal because of the inner forces that work against it. Or, alternatively, we achieve our conscious goal but don't feel satisfied, because the underlying, unexpressed need has not been met. There is still something missing. Either way, we get the feeling of failure – a pretty good sign that we have failed.

This is where you need the self-knowledge of knowing what you want. It doesn't require a superior intellect. But it does demand focus and a level of self-knowledge you may not have sought in the past. It also requires some basic know-how and simple steps:

- list your goals;
- apply SMART criteria (see the next page);
- express your goal in positive terms;
- make your goals sensory;
- align your goals;
- allow for other people;
- ask goal-testing questions.

You don't need special skills to carry out these goal-setting steps. You can improve your intrapersonal intelligence *just by doing them*, in your own common sense way.

In fact, you may find that you do these things anyway *without thinking*. That's fine, but part of self-knowledge is to understand *how* you think and use your mind to direct your behaviour in a more purposeful way. However, in most cases extra know-how will make the process more effective. This is especially the case when you need to tap into your unconscious mind, if you have not been in the habit of doing so. You will get the extra know-how, or 'goal technology' you need in this part of the chapter.

List your goals

Start by listing all your goals, desires, wishes, hopes, dreams, intentions and whatever. Do this quickly and intuitively without questioning the common sense or even the possibility of what you include. Put these into clear language, as choosing the words helps you express what you want more clearly. Your list need not be in any order or ranking. Include both long- and short-term goals. Include those that have little chance of becoming reality as well as those you feel sure about achieving.

Apply SMART criteria

Check these against the well-known SMART criteria. This will reduce your goals to a serious, practicable shortlist and form the basis of your important purpose: self-knowledge.

Specific

Your goal should be so specific that you can't make excuses if you fail. Achievement or non-achievement will be obvious. A non-specific or ambiguous goal, however laudable (like, 'I want to be happy') doesn't really register in your unconscious mind where it matters. For instance, what exactly do you mean by being 'happy'. Or, what specific achievement or event will make you feel happy? Ask yourself, 'What, specifically, do I mean by ...?'

Measurable

There is more chance of making a goal specific if you have some yardstick or measure of success. You will be able to register a clear hit or miss, and you will also be able to measure the degree to which you achieved your goal – your percentage success, if you like. In other cases, measurement will give *evidence* of what you have (or haven't) attained. If you have set yourself a goal of reaching a certain weight, for example, what is better than actually weighing yourself to prove you fulfilled your goal? Similarly, if your goal is an academic one, what better measure of success than an 'A' grade on your marked assignment, or a distinction in your examination? Some goals can only be measured in quality, rather than quantity, of course. However, *any* attempt to make your goals measurable will increase your motivation and chances of success. Note that you can measure by time also – by when or within however many weeks or months you will achieve your goal.

Achievable

You will do yourself no favours by aiming too high. Having

said that, most of us underestimate our potential, and in general aim far too low. That may mean we are not motivated enough. Your goal-achieving mind enjoys a challenge, and there is pleasure each time we reach a new level of achievement. What is 'achievable' is personal, of course. It will depend on your age, knowledge, experience to date, state of health and so on. But bear in mind that all kinds of resources – inner and outer – can be acquired and improved in the longer term. You can add new knowledge and skills. You can gain experience a bit at a time, just as you can get into physical shape with a gradual programme of exercise. Achievement may be what you can *make happen*, rather than what you do personally. We can all call upon the intelligence to raise our 'achievable' sights and fulfil our true potential. Put another way, 'achievable', is what each of us makes it.

Realistic

Again, set this in context. What would have been realistic ten years ago is maybe not now. What might be a realistic goal within five years might not be realistic – given your other goals and priorities – in one year. There are no finite measures, of course, but the simple act of thinking about the things you want in this structured way will easily repay the time and effort.

Timely

Timeliness also depends on what else you hope to achieve, and the relative importance you place on each goal. Something you could easily achieve in six months might take second place if it conflicts with important family or other demands. Timing will usually be a factor in any goal setting. Adding a timescale can make a goal more specific and measurable. Similarly, the deadline you set for yourself can make a goal achievable and realistic, or render it unachievable and unrealistic. Set at the right level, it provides the essential degree of challenge and motivation. Intelligent people use time as an important resource in their life. There is usually a trade-off between long and short-term goals, and long and short-term effort and cost. Paradoxically, the busiest people seem to make time. Include it as an important variable in every goal you set. Treat time as an asset rather than a liability, a servant rather than a master.

Express your goal in positive terms

That doesn't just mean 'thinking positively', but actually expressing, or 'framing' your goal in positive language. For instance, to 'reach a weight of nine stone', rather than to 'lose half a stone'. The difference may seem innocuous, but it is important in terms of the way your unconscious goal-achieving mechanisms work. The words you use are important. As a golfer, do you want to reach the flag in two (hit), or avoid the tree, water and bunkers (miss)? Thinking what you *don't* want – especially if it is graphic and easily imaginable like trees and bunkers – sets up an ideal image for your unconscious mind to aim for. So – surprise, surprise – you 'achieve' what was uppermost in your mind in a remarkable, self-fulfilling way. An internal image, whether positive or negative, becomes reality, however hard you 'think' and try. We are all free to call a glass half-full or half-empty. An optimistic attitude requires no less effort than a pessimistic attitude. And, as it happens, not only will it produce more successes, but it's a more enjoyable process whether you ultimately succeed or not. If you happen to prefer pleasure to pain, that is an intelligent approach to take.

Make your goals sensory

Clothe every goal with sights, sounds and feelings. That is, with the stuff of 'sensory reality'. Visualize your outcome as you intend to actually experience it. Visualization of this sort crops up in all sorts of situations, such as creativity, problem solving, setting priorities, scenario planning, self-motivation and so on. It is also useful as a mental test to determine what is realistic and achieveable, and for 'foretasting', or 'pre-experiencing' an otherwise abstract, non-sensory goal. Once again, you don't need a higher degree in sensory acuity. We do it when daydreaming about an upcoming holiday, or indeed when savouring any pleasurable goal – and without prompting or special training. It's a natural thing, as is all human intelligence. To use such a faculty consciously, or purposefully, just takes desire, practice and the usual generous measure of common sense. In short, it's up to you how compelling and pleasurable you make your goals. Just use your imagination.

An important use of visualization, or mental (sensory) rehearsal, is to get a realistic experience of what it will be like to actually achieve a desire. That 'experience' or mental preview may not turn out to be what you had hoped for. There are downsides. Other things in your life and in relationships may be affected which you would not have foreseen without deliberate sensory 'testing'. All this is invaluable self-knowledge, and the skill of visualization, or mental rehearsal, a part of the intrapersonal intelligence package. With the right positive, learning attitude, the lessons you learn from *imagined* failure will prove to be invaluable, and you will incorporate them into future goal setting. The simple principles in this chapter might save you a few years of wasted effort and disappointment. To be more intelligent just means to start thinking, not just cognitively, or abstractly, but in a sensory, emotional way.

Align your goals

Some of your goals, after applying the SMART criteria, will turn out to be mutually incompatible. Career goals, for instance, can, and often do, conflict with family life and relationships – and vice versa. In that case something has to give. However, by giving this thought up front, not only will you avoid failing in one (or often both) goals, but you may be able to make them compatible with relatively small changes (such as delaying for a period, or adjusting your target slightly).

Sometimes we pursue goals that we are not conscious of, and thus can be a cause of conflict. However, as you *consciously* apply the checks in this chapter you will find that these underlying motives and intentions will pop to the surface. 'Sleeping on the matter' produces a similar exposure of hidden thoughts.

Allow for other people

Not only do you need to get your various goals and desires aligned, but also you may need to get them aligned with other people's goals and interests, if such people are important in your life. Succeeding in your own goals, at the expense of others you care about, may not bring the expected pleasure of success.

That doesn't mean that you have to fulfil other people's goals, which is beyond our reasonable ability anyway. It is important to confine yourself to outcomes that you will have reasonable control over. There may well be specific things you can do to help somebody reach *their* goals. That's fine, as you can make such specific assistance or support your *own goal*. We each have our own desires and lives to live, and there is a fundamental law which says that we can't abrogate our own purposes, or fulfil someone else's.

Ask goal-testing questions

Asking goal-testing questions such as the following will help to sort your priorities and establish important, self-motivating goals:

- Am I sure I really want this?
- What will I get once I have reached my outcome?

- What do I really want?
- How will my life differ, having achieved this outcome?
- How will I integrate this outcome into my present life?
- What will it mean to me to have this outcome?
- Would this outcome seem appropriate in every situation?
- What effect will it have on my life?
- What will happen after I achieve my goal?
- What advantages will result from my achieving it?
- What impact will achieving this have on the rest of my life?
- What would *not* happen if I achieved this?
- What would happen if I *didn't* achieve it?
- What would *not* happen if I didn't achieve it?
- Are there other areas of my life where achieving this outcome could have benefits or disadvantages?
- How do I see this outcome as important?

After applying these different goal criteria, you may well finish up with a considerably reduced list of goals. That's fine. You have a far better chance of achieving those you are left with, and – more than that – you will get more pleasure and a greater sense of fulfilment as you achieve them. With a bit of ingenuity you may find that you don't need to sacrifice any of your important goals, nor the values you hold important. It just means channelling your mind and energy towards more meaningful things.

Knowing what is important

Not only will your goals become clearer and less conflicting as you follow these guidelines, but you will at the same tend to reappraise your values. Goals you give thought to, and the values that underlie them, will find their own pecking order of importance.

Your goals and values are interdependent, of course. They *are* 'you'. Emotional literacy means they are in harmony, heading in the same direction. Each will affect the other. For instance, your values will be reflected in what you aim for in life – what you want. Similarly, in pursuing what you want, part of your criteria for success will be adhering to your values.

Your goals and values, in turn, will also be mutually affected by the five characteristics of intrapersonal intelligence we met earlier. For instance, our goals will include feelings – what we want to *feel* as well as what we want to *get*, *do*, etc. Similarly, our emotions are inevitably wrapped up in our values (what is important to us). We invariably want to get from one *state* (such as unhappy) to another *state* (such as happy or content). The desire to be happy, inherent in most of our goals, is a state of mind – a feeling. Our desire for self-actualization, or fulfilment, is usually wrapped up in our purposes and goals in life. In the same way we assert ourselves in an attempt to get what we want – that is, for a purpose. Emotional literacy means balance and harmony between all these intrapersonal aspects of our life, on the basis of what is important to us.

In this section we will concentrate on values. These usually become apparent as we carry out the SMART and other goal exercises, especially when giving priority to one goal over another, and considering other people. However, you can also identify your values in a more direct, positive way.

Identifying your values

A value is what is important to you. If you have as a value 'honesty', it means you consider it important to be honest. Your value is also an underlying goal, or intention ('I want to be honest'). All your goals have to be compatible with this value, or you will not experience the sense of achievement and pleasure you hoped for in pursuing a specific goal, however sincerely and single-mindedly.

Thus, each goal you identify will have to be checked against your 'honesty' value – and any other personal values. In the process of identifying and reassessing your values you may identify further unconscious intentions, so you will further refine your short list of goals.

Here's how to identify your values. Divide your life into main categories – such as work, social, family and home, self. Then ask yourself, in the context of each category, 'What is important to me?'

For example, starting with work/career. What is important to you about your job? Freedom? Meeting people? Variety? Using your mind? Just write down the word or words that come to mind. Then ask the question again, applying it to your answer. 'What is important to me about freedom (meeting people, variety and so on)?' Again write down what instinctively comes to your mind. For example:

Freedom: 'true to myself', 'can be creative', 'use my mind'.

Meeting people: 'broadening my mind', 'learning', 'making relationships'.

Ask the question again: What is important to me about broadening my mind ...? Answer, for example, 'living up to my full potential' and so on. Carry on in this way until either you completely run out of answers, or you start stating the same things again – ie going round in circles.

Do the same exercise for each of the main categories of your life. For instance: 'In my family and home life, what is important to me?' Answer: 'honesty', 'faithfulness', 'relationships', and so on. You may be surprised at how a shortlist of 'importance factors' recurs in every part of your life. This is simply because you are the same person even when in different roles. We don't abandon important values with every change in day-to-day happenings.

This shortlist of values is important self-knowledge. It clarifies what you want in life, why your behaviour has followed certain patterns, why you are in the job you are in, have the friends and partner you have, and are interested in certain things and not in others. It is an important aspect of intrapersonal intelligence.

A handful of 'important things' will keep recurring, and these are your values. They play a big part in everything you do. Note that you may never in the past have identified these in such a conscious, deliberate way. However, by knowing them you will probably understand better your behaviour, and why you tend to do well in some things (that fit your values) and not in others (that don't). In other words, you will identify how your values, acting like unconscious intentions or forces on your life, affect your goals and outcomes – what you achieve. You always have the choice, of course, to changes your values, or your goals, or both.

Aligning your goals and values

You can now check-off each of your outcomes, or goals – after making the SMART changes earlier – in the light of your values. For example, how does so-and-so goal fit my value of 'independence', 'family relationships' or whatever? You can be certain that any outcome you pursue that runs contrary to your 'system' of values (a hierarchy of important, not-so-important, etc) will not have much chance of success. Moreover, the successes you do chalk up will not seem to give the pleasure and sense of fulfilment that you would have hoped for. If you like, it turns out that that was not what you really wanted. Now that you know why, you can realign your goals and behaviour in such a way that better reflects your values – what is important to you. Identifying any conflict between your values and your outcomes is the intelligent approach if you want to clock up successes and enjoy them when you do.

Knowing what you feel

This aspect of intelligence involves more self-awareness. As well as knowing what you want, and what is important to you, you need to be aware of your feelings, and how they may affect what you do and in turn what you achieve. Unless you feel right, just about any goal can be ruined even before you start. For instance, without motivation, an important emotion, you might not get round to starting, let alone finishing something important in your life.

Knowing how you feel is the easy part. At any time you can probably say, in a word or two, how you feel. Even if you cannot put your finger on a proper kind of emotion, you will no doubt come up with an expression – like 'lousy', or 'really on form' that sufficiently identifies the emotion in quality or degree. That is not to say that you will know *why* you feel that way. Like some of the other aspects of thinking that make up intelligence, this operates as effectively 'below the surface'. In short, there may be no rhyme nor reason for this major factor in anything we do and achieve.

The smart trick with feelings is using them, controlling them, to support what you know you want to do, get or be. Values and internal goals and outcomes play their part in directing our behaviour towards those goals and values. Whilst feelings may operate on a shorter timescale (the slightest distraction can change the way we feel) they are nonetheless crucial to our competence right now, when it matters.

The common sense questions to ask are therefore:

- Which feelings are useful?
- How can I evoke those feelings when it would be helpful to do so?

Feelings which don't suit your requirements don't figure in this. That is, if you're smart, you will not pay them undue attention, other than to replace them with more useful ones. As with goals, it's what you want rather than what you don't want that matters.

Some feelings, you may decide are always of use and they are empowering. That is, they invariably help you to achieve whatever goals you set yourself. Confidence, self-esteem and optimism might fit that 'empowering', positive category. Others may be of use in some situations, but not in others, so it's 'horses for courses'. Excitement will sometimes help, whilst at other times it may be better to stay, for example, cool, 'low-key' or calm. It depends on what you want to achieve and the different circumstances – not least the actual people involved. Anger can be useful on the odd occasion, as can a 'couldn't care less' attitude or childish, 'fun' emotions. Fortunately, as humans we all experience the whole gamut of emotions, even as children, so we have a pretty comprehensive inner, emotional database to call upon. That means you know what it means to feel 'confident', 'calm', 'proud' or whatever. All that remains, therefore, is to be able to recall (remember, if you like) an emotional memory. Bearing in mind that emotions actually help to create strong memories (our earliest memories are usually 'emotionally memorable'), this is easier than maths or history memory work.

Here's how it works. If you want to be carefree, think back to a time when you were carefree. Re-live that experience, and all the emotion that went with it. Do this vividly, realistically, *seriously*. This means that you see, hear, and feel the actual experience. The emotions will come as part of the multi-sensory memory 'package' as you evoke each of the senses.

These emotions are your resources, to be used when and how you decide to use them. Using this memory device (which is a skill, and gets better with practice), you can not only identify and isolate specific feelings, but you can capture them as well. That means you feel now – or whenever you need to – what you felt then.

Try it. With a little practice you will soon be able to recall an emotion within moments. Each time you access that emotion, recall will become quicker, easier and more realistic. Before long you will simply *think* 'calm', 'confident' or whatever. By adding 'state control' to your personal goal and value self-knowledge, you can increase your intrapersonal intelligence to a remarkable degree. These are the main factors, and they are readily learnable. If you want to reach a higher level in this aspect of emotional intelligence you can learn about 'anchoring' empowering states in this author's book entitled *NLP in 21 Days*.

It is wise to never stop learning. It is wiser to never stop self-learning. Self-learning is intrapersonal intelligence. As you apply it to setting and pursuing goals, identifying and aligning your values with those goals, and managing your state of mind, you can convert this kind of intelligence into all manner of goodies in your life.

4

Getting on with others: interpersonal intelligence

People with a high interpersonal intelligence are 'people people'. They understand, interact, and relate well with others. Others, in turn, will usually consider them 'dependable', 'responsible' and 'personable'. In work settings, they perform well in teams and interact successfully with customers, colleagues, and bosses. In this chapter you will learn about what is sometimes called social intelligence, with some techniques for improving your interpersonal communication skills.

Social intelligence

Interpersonal intelligence concerns the social 'you'. It involves:

- understanding others;

- social competence;
- relationship know-how.

Understanding others

Being aware of and appreciating other people's feelings is central to emotional intelligence. We sometimes call it empathy. We witness it in statements such as 'I can just imagine how you must have felt.' It means seeing the world as if through another person's eyes. It means being able to 'read' other people's emotions, and to make allowances for them in what we say and do. Empathy, another ability that builds on emotional self-awareness, is the fundamental 'people skill'. People who have empathy are more attuned to the subtle social signals that indicate what others need or want. This makes them better at careers such as the caring professions, teaching, sales, and management. This is part of interpersonal intelligence.

These are the sorts of questions that will help you check out your own empathy rating:

- Are you sensitive to the feelings of other people?
- Are you a good listener?
- Can you quickly grasp how people feel, and why they feel as they do?
- Can you 'read' other people's emotions, from their body language and voice tone as well as their words?

Empathy is strongly related to the intrapersonal skill of knowing your own feelings that we looked at in Chapter 3. It starts with you. It is not hard to understand how a person might feel as a result of certain behaviour if you have experienced that yourself. Better still if you can *imagine* what you would have felt, whatever your own experience. That is the emotional competence of empathy.

Understanding how a person feels need not dictate how you

act. Being a good listener, for instance, doesn't mean that you have to agree with everything you listen to, or not get your point of view across. However, the benefit of understanding others better is that you have more *knowledge* on which to make decisions, more *choices* as to how you behave, and a better chance of communicating well and forming good relationships.

In empathizing, you can share your own feelings, if you wish. You can be assertive and independent without riding roughshod over other people. You can take others into account when fixing your goals. You can handle problems involving people (which most do) more effectively and more intelligently. Behaviour is usually more effective where there is empathy.

Social intelligences apply universally, and are not confined to a part of your life or a certain type of behaviour. However, this intelligence characteristic usually applies to relationships with family, friends, work colleagues and such, rather than with passing strangers. It is within closer relationships that we commonly face problems and share feelings, and it is these cases that most affect our own goals.

We sometimes need to learn or relearn these social competencies. However, as with the other types of intelligence you have met, they are *learnable* and *do-able*. For instance, you may have to consciously and deliberately listen more, and seek another perspective or reframe a situation. Or you may ask yourself specific questions such as 'How must she feel?' or 'What if I was in his position?'. Interpersonal social traits are invariably habits, and habits can be changed, but not without commitment and conscious effort. A habit, once established, is more or less maintenance free, so it's worth applying yourself to make the change. You may need to acquire particular know-how such as in this book, but otherwise simply *doing* what you now know is do-able will start the important process of change.

Social competence

This aspect of interpersonal intelligence extends beyond your personal friends, family and work colleagues. It involves wider social groups and the community generally. 'Socially intelligent' people have what we might call a 'social consciousness', 'social literacy' and a basic concern for others. Ask yourself the following kinds of question:

- Am I a cooperative, constructive team player?
- Would others say I am responsible and dependable?
- Do I do things for and with people because it is right to do so?
- Do I act according to my conscience?

We say of a person with social competence, 'he can get along with anyone', or 'she is a really likeable person' (meaning: 'she is nice, courteous, honest, etc with *me*. I like her'). The skill extends to communicating across cultures, and tolerance of people who are different in any respect to you. This requires *knowledge* (such as of a national or organization culture, customs and more) and *skills* (in conducting yourself in a socially intelligent way). Both can be learnt, and both will add to your social competence.

Such behaviour calls for a high self-worth: you accept yourself as you are; you have nothing to 'prove' (to the world or to yourself); you are happy in and satisfied in *yourself*. As with empathy, it depends on your intrapersonal intelligence: knowing yourself.

Interpersonal skills make for better organizations and businesses. 'Social responsibility' is the minimum most customers look for in their dealings with salespeople, service staff, and other front-line employees. However, extensive customer service training projects often flounder, because the attitudes of staff are not changed. Inner, intrapersonal attitudes remain untouched, so any outward behaviour and 'scripts' are quickly exposed as insincere. The bottom line is clear: not only is intelligence more than intellectual ability and IQ, but it is more than the words and outward behaviour we usually associate with 'customer service', 'team spirit' and the like. Rules of behaviour are not enough, however well intentioned. Emotional intelligence is more to do with *being* than either doing or knowing.

Relationship know-how

One aspect of interpersonal intelligence is the ability to create and enjoy mutually satisfying relationships. Many problems are people problems. Usually, it's not *what* is the problem, but *who*? Invariably a problem will have more to do with the relationship dimensions of what's going on than with the technical issues. This applies equally in work, family or social situations.

Interpersonal skills, such as being able to 'read people's feelings', are important for day-to-day and *ad hoc* dealings with others, and good relationships depend on them. But whatever 'people' skills you possess, the real test is in the quality of relationships formed and maintained, especially long-term, meaningful ones. When you get this right, others will like being around you, and find the relationship rewarding and enjoyable. It involves both giving and receiving appropriate affection and respect. It means that both parties can 'be themselves', just as in a family relationship. You will know a person has a high EQ in this area because you will feel at ease and comfortable around them. They won't embarrass you or put you on the spot. They emanate warmth and openness, or 'transparency'. Here are the sorts of self-assessment questions you can ask yourself:

- Are you capable of having mutually satisfying relationships?
- Are you able to be comfortable around people, of all types and classes?
- Would you say you have excellent human relations skills?

There is probably nothing as important in life as having good relationships. Feeling significant or important to someone who is important to us, like a partner, colleague, boss or family member, is a basic human need. When a relationship is not working well, it is the basis for much pain, stress and, often, illness. We can't live out emotional literacy as an island, which is why many high-IQ 'loners' fail despite their enviable intellect. In measuring success in terms of career, social interests and fulfilling interests and hobbies, the ability to form relationships is crucial. Naturally introverted people also require this emotional foundation, even though, for them, it may apply to a very small number of important relationships.

Relationships can spell success or failure in many different contexts. The smart way is to make relationships work *for* you, not *against* you. We can call this 'relationship know-how'. You can't assume you have 'got it' in the way that you can speak your mother tongue, climb stairs and drink coffee without spilling it. Whilst these are learnt competencies, success in mature relationships usually demands a lot of conscious thinking and specific behaviour. Successful, long-term relationships have to be fostered and maintained.

We all have the potential for satisfying relationships, and genetic deficiencies are no excuse. A person with a low EQ can increase it significantly in a couple of months – that's what this book is about. Change is possible. So a 'relationship' self-label is no more relevant than a supposedly fixed IQ. Brain software, rather than hardware, is what matters. And the good news about brain software is that we can design it, run it and manage it ourselves. In short, we can think as we want to think and 'change our mind' if we care to. There's nothing too technical. For instance, you may need to:

- recognize your limitation and need for knowledge or skills;
- change your attitude when necessary;
- change your self-beliefs;

- use your goal technology to reach personal relationship goals;
- practice listening, observing and imagining how others feel.

You can start by understanding yourself better, and developing your interpersonal intelligence as we saw in the previous chapter. Be honest with yourself in answering the questions earlier in this chapter. With such a foundation of self-knowledge and consideration for others, the specific communication skills in the remainder of this chapter will enable you to aspire to mastery in this part of your emotional intelligence.

Communicating to get results

Interpersonal intelligence comprises what we sometimes call people skills. It is about interpersonal communication, forming relationships and understanding others. As with most of the emotional intelligence traits we are considering, is seems that some of these characteristics come with the *nature* ('you're born that way') package. For instance, a person with an extrovert personality will find it much easier to communicate than an introvert, and will probably do it much better. As ever, however, nurture plays its part. Someone from a large family, or a younger sibling, or a child who attended playgroups and nursery school, will probably have better-developed interpersonal skills than an only child who has had less exposure to other children.

Fortunately, interpersonal skills can be learnt at any age. Salespeople, for instance, after proper training, are often much more competent at getting along with people generally, as well as performing better in their job technically. Training is similarly effective in negotiation, counselling, public speaking, teaching, interviewing and other skills that fall in this interpersonal intelligence category. So even with a natural slow start or seeming lack in people skills, there is plenty of scope for improving this part of your emotional intelligence. Put simply, *anyone* can be more socially intelligent, at any stage in life and – for all practical purposes – to any degree.

Many personal characteristics, talents, specific skills, experience and bigger environmental factors such as upbringing and education go to make up this kind of social intelligence. So we need to, first, decide which to concentrate on, and second, learn the principles and techniques that will produce the biggest improvement.

The main skills to go for are probably 'getting on easily' and 'having a genuine interest in people' and establishing warm, mature relationships. Often empathy, sensitivity, a sense of humour, openness and rapport are cited. This is largely covered by the term interpersonal communication. This includes non-verbal communication, of course, an important characteristic of interpersonal intelligence. Interpersonal communication is a two way process, a 'meeting of minds'.

Rapport is a word that encompasses much of what interpersonal communication is about. It involves mutual interest and trust and what is sometimes called positive 'chemistry'. Typically, when we get it right, we might say 'we just seem to hit it off from the start'. This may happen by default, with no rhyme or reason as to who we hit it off with and who we don't. The trick (requiring no mean interpersonal intelligence) is to positively create rapport when you feel it is in your interest (purpose) to do so.

Matching

An important principle in interpersonal skills is that of matching, or creating the perception of 'likeness'. 'She is my kind of person' often transpires to mean 'She is *like me*' (in values, interests, etc). In fact, the principle of matching has been found to be a factor in many aspects of interpersonal communication. For example, matching (or 'mirroring'):

- posture and body language;
- voice (tone, pitch and speed);
- goals (common objectives);
- values (agreement on what is important);
- interests and experience (having had common experiences, done similar things).

Wherever we see rapport in action – say two people locked into absorbing conversation – we will probably witness some of these matching characteristics. Conversely, *mismatching* usually indicates poor communication. Matching happens quite unconsciously, of course, as with all habitual behaviours.

Imagine this not uncommon scenario. One person sits, immobile, with crossed arms and legs, speaking in a slow, steady tone of voice with a deadpan, poker face. The other person is animated, speaks quickly, in a high-pitched voice, leans forward, smiles and gesticulates heavily. With such mismatching, there is probably not much positive chemistry at work, and precious little real communication, or 'meeting of minds'. Moreover, the outcomes – or intentions – of the communicator in the duo (say a salesperson, negotiator or manager) are unlikely to be fulfilled. In a word, the communication is *ineffective*, whatever the correctness of the words used or the sincere intention of the parties. More to the point, if an outcome (that is, whatever was intended through the communication) is not achieved, the communicator is not displaying much interpersonal intelligence.

Failure is often put down to saying the wrong thing, the content of the communication (say the price in a negotiation, or the terms in a job interview, or a difference of opinion) or the intention, attitude and even integrity of the other party ('it's their fault'). Yet however we rationalize a failed communication, if we don't learn from experience, but repeat our failure, we are not emotionally literate. In short, interpersonal communication behaviour that consistently fails to communicate is dumb, whoever is to 'blame'.

Rapport is a natural, intuitive feature of good interpersonal communication. We are not taught it, in the way we are taught much cognitive 'intelligence', such as language and maths. However, we need not despair in matters of social competence, even after many years of failure. We can create rapport consciously and purposefully by adhering to certain matching principles, and learning the techniques of matching posture, voice tone, etc listed earlier.

In the above example, the communicator (whoever wanted to bring about some outcome through or with the other person – to convince, sell to, placate, motivate, etc) might have moderated their own behaviour, deliberately slowing down and mirroring the general body language of the other person. By matching the other person's behaviour, we create 'likeness'.

Even more basically, the communicator could have established a clear *purpose* in the communication. With a clear objective in mind we are more likely to choose appropriate (goal-oriented) behaviour, and will then stand a better chance of success.

The SMART goal principles introduced in Chapter 3 apply to any kind of goal, including a communication, such as an interview, sales pitch, one-to-one meeting, negotiation and so on. In this case, *intrapersonal* intelligence reaps benefits in *interpersonal* situations. As with any type of intelligence, its effect on our lives is far-reaching. In fact, just by thinking about what you want out of the communication (one aspect only of intelligent goal setting) you are well on the way to success. Put another way, with intelligent preparation you are more likely to adopt effective behaviour.

Pacing and leading

The tendency to match is so strong where there is rapport that a conscious change of behaviour on the part of one person will usually produce a matching response. For instance, when you are in rapport, and a conversation is in 'flow', one party can deliberately change the tone and speed of the communication, perhaps to encourage a more serious, reflective level, more conducive to the purpose of the communication. Similarly, you can foster a more light-hearted tone by changing your body language and voice characteristics, whilst maintaining the positive rapport already achieved.

The new 'tone' of the communication will be automatically, unknowingly adopted by the other person.

By first pacing (matching) then leading, by changing your behaviour, a communicator can bring about real, physiological changes in the other party. By inducing a state of mind (such as 'calm', 'alert', 'impressed') conducive to the objective in the communication (such as coming to a decision, gaining agreement or support, eliciting help or advice or whatever), a successful outcome is all but certain. For instance, you may want a person to calm down, be less serious, or more attentive. Each state has its preferred body language and voice characteristics and by leading the person to adopt these you will have a better chance of achieving what you want to achieve through the communication.

The principle of pacing and leading is simple, and reflects what the best communicators do without being aware of it. An extraordinary degree of skill can be attained in these interpersonal techniques, with equally extraordinary results.

Keep a few things in mind when considering matching:

- Anyone can 'match' and thus improve their interpersonal competence.
- You don't have to have an outgoing personality or special disposition. Even if you don't aspire to being the best, you can expect to see a remarkable improvement, just going 'part-way' will bring effects.
- Matching should be used as a genuine strategy for successful communication rather than a contrived

technique designed to manipulate or unduly coerce – it's easier to fake a maths test than body language.

- Any interpersonal skill is best used from the foundation of a high self-esteem. Start with yourself before the other party. Start with the inside (attitude) before the outside (behaviour). This is where intra- and interpersonal skills combine to form emotional literacy.
- Don't be put off by early failures. Human interpersonal skills are awesomely complex and have to be learnt as with any worthwhile ability. You will improve your skill with practice.

Mismatching

You can use the same principles to *mismatch*, in cases where, for whatever reason, you want to bring a communication to an end. By consciously, gratuitously changing your body language and voice characteristics, you will tend to break rapport. The other person, unaware of this, will find it difficult to carry on with what will seem like a one-sided communication. This is a useful skill at a party or social gathering when you want to move away from someone, or when you want to escape from an enthusiastic salesperson without giving offence. Senior managers and chairpersons sometimes use mismatching to great effect to bring a meeting or interview to a summary close. Even the subtlest mismatch can instantly kill a conversation. Try, for instance, repeatedly glancing over a person's shoulder at a social event, half-glancing at your watch, or simply looking glazedly *through* your co-communicator into the mid-distance.

Used positively and knowingly, mismatching is an example of high EQ behaviour. The skill is in producing a mismatch without spoiling a relationship, causing offence, or failing to achieve your overall communication intention. The other person need not be conscious of what has happened other than it 'didn't seem right' to carry on communicating. You can improve such people skills to a degree equivalent to a 150 IQ if you are ready to learn, and change your attitudes and self-beliefs when needed.

The desire and ability to communicate better is the main characteristic of interpersonal intelligence. Having identified the factors involved by answering the questions, and applying them in a common sense way in your life, you will boost your emotional intelligence and enjoy real successes in your life. Technical training, such as in selling or negotiation skills, will produce a marked improvement, so you are not stuck with any hereditary traits or seemingly immutable tendencies. On the contrary, you can do a lot on a DIY basis, applying the simple principles you have learnt. You can learn more about matching, in specific situations such as meetings, in this author's various NLP books.

The matching know-how you can get from this chapter is just one example of skills that will boost your emotional intelligence. Part of emotional intelligence is to spot where change is needed (self-knowledge) and seek out whatever resources will help you achieve your purpose of self-actualization and personal fulfilment. Resources may be:

- information, such as from books or the Internet;
- your own knowledge and skills you can bring to bear on a situation;
- new skills you have the learning resources to acquire;
- people who will help;
- your inner resources of commitment, self-esteem, motivation and purpose.

Thankfully, there is much more help available to brush up interpersonal skills than to increase your IQ, as you learnt in Chapter 2. So you can choose the level of interpersonal intelligence to which you want to aspire and start to take control of your own improvement.

5

Boosting your EQ

There are no standard, validated EQ tests, so there isn't much need for test sophistication of the sort described in Chapter 2. However, emotional intelligence can be improved, whether measured or not. Even more importantly, the changes you make in emotional intelligence will probably have a significant effect on your life.

Daniel Goleman describes five critical skills of emotional intelligence in his popular book *Emotional Intelligence*. These are based on five 'domains' identified by Mayer and Salovey, who introduced EI:

- knowing your emotions;
- managing your emotions;
- motivating yourself;
- recognizing emotion in others;
- handling relationships.

These approximately equate to the intra- and interpersonal intelligences we covered in Chapters 3 and 4, two of the multiple intelligences that Howard Gardner described. EI, however, includes managing as well as knowing your emotions, one of the intrapersonal traits ('emotional self-awareness') we have also met. It includes self-motivation as a separate critical skill.

Other elements of EI are popularly used, and in this chapter we will address:

- handling stress;
- controlling impulse;
- managing moods.

A section on 'EQ at work' has been included, which is a popular aspect of EQ. You will have a chance to answer some typical EQ questions in a test at the end of the chapter.

Handling stress

Stress is a much-quoted ailment of modern life in work, home and social situations. The pace of technology, the scale and emotional impact of company downsizing, job insecurity, restructuring and ubiquitous change all play their part. Lots of books have been written on the subject and advice is readily available.

'Stress tolerance' is the ability to withstand adverse events and stressful situations without falling apart. It means positively managing the stress, and turning it to good effect. It means:

- being resourceful in coming up with ways of handling and diffusing stress before it can do damage;
- remaining effective at work, at home and in one's personal life even when faced with adverse circumstances and even trauma;
- staying on an 'even keel';
- the ability to ride life's difficulties positively;
- understanding the way different things cause stress to you personally and learning to spot them and regulate their effect;

- having what is called 'ego strength' or 'emotional resilience';
- coming to terms with change, and having mastery over its effect on your life.

High scorers on this EQ factor face difficulties head on, and don't get carried away by strong emotions. It is an invaluable mental trait that can be cultivated in the school of hard experience. It is almost a necessity in today's changing workplaces and the decline of close family life. Change is a fact of life for most of us, and pressure of different kinds is part of the package.

Yet there is immense variance between people as regards what causes stress and how it affects our lives. What causes stress in one person will mean pleasure, or 'a challenge' to another. Some people seem addicted to stressful situations and behaviours. Some actually thrive on it, and produce their best work under pressure.

People who 'score' high on this intelligence scale tend to handle what life throws at them. They can 'roll with the punches'. They stay in control. They may fall, but they don't stay down. With their full share of life's stressful events (and sometimes, it seems, more), they do not fall apart.

Apply each of the above factors to yourself by asking 'Is this me?' A checklist of questions may also help:

- Do you handle adverse events well?
- Do you manage frustration effectively?
- Do you live life so as not to create a feeling of 'overload'?
- Do you cope well in new situations, with significant unknown factors?
- Do you usually minimize anxiety to avoid feeling stuck?
- Do you generally get a good night's sleep?
- Are you able to hold back comments in a disagreement even though you feel your stress level rising?

- Do you cope well with daily events that can sometimes be frustrating?
- Would colleagues and friends say you manage your anger well? How about your family?
- Do you cope well with disappointment?

Stress is something that happens inside, and is rarely just the effect of outside circumstances and life events. This becomes obvious when we observe how people handle outside circumstances very differently. It involves thinking patterns, habits, beliefs, values and the different components of intrapersonal intelligence we have already met.

We can start to manage it by first being aware of its ubiquitous presence and adverse effects, then by considering it as part of the goal-setting, value-fixing processes we met in Chapter 3.

A number of proven techniques will help.

Reframing

This means looking for different meanings, different perspectives, pros as well as cons, opportunities, lessons we can learn, serendipity and so on – a different frame of reference. Any experience will cause pleasure or pain depending on how we perceive it. The ability to consciously change our perceptions, by 'imagining' another meaning, a different outcome, or taking a new perspective, is part of this intrapersonal mental skill. You can improve this using the goal-setting and other self-knowledge processes you met in Chapter 3, and some of the creativity skills you will meet in Chapter 6.

Relaxation and deep breathing

There is no shortage of books and resources on this topic, whose effectiveness has been well proven in many areas of human behaviour. There are also local night class courses and self-help groups for those who don't like to work on their own. For those who can easily relax in a hobby, with a good book, or listening to music, it is hard to understand how difficult it can be for some people to turn off. Some people seem constantly 'driven' and find it impossible to relax and 'turn off'. Hence the need for specific, deliberate learning, drawing on the wide range of resources available. Meditation, yoga, and a range of sports can help in alleviating stress. Relaxation and deep breathing are just examples of stress-reducing techniques that anyone can benefit from.

Visualization

Thankfully, we can usually think back to times when we did not experience stress, perhaps on holiday, in a previous job or when younger. Indeed, we can usually recall pleasant, relaxed and confident times, which reflect just the mental state we need in our present situation. Such memories are important resources we can all call upon. By visually, vividly recalling the experience, we will invoke the positive, empowering state associated with it, and instantly reduce present stress. If need be, we can 'anchor' such positive states so that they are instantly available (this author's book *NLP in 21 Days* covers this subject in some depth). The point is that there are things you can *do* about stress, if need be by learning a skill such as relaxation and deep breathing. Willingness to learn and commitment to change are features of emotional intelligence and offer unlimited scope for improving your life.

Controlling impulses

This is the emotional characteristic that allows a person to delay gratification.

The so-called 'marshmallow test' illustrates emotional

regulation, or 'state control', well. This is a test Walter Mischel, a Columbia University researcher, carried out on four-year-old children. He took a child into a room with a marshmallow on a plate, and told them (cruelly), 'You can have this now, but if you wait till I come back you can have two marshmallows.' Hidden cameras recorded the critical behaviour. Some children summarily ate the single treat. Others held out for minutes, then gave in. Others were determined to wait, even singing, covering their eyes, playing games – even sleeping – to withstand the temptation. These were rewarded with the extra marshmallow.

The marshmallow test turned out to be a significant factor in the intelligence of the children. Following their progress through school, a significant correlation was found between holding out for the second treat and academic success. Moreover, the stoic group were also better adjusted, happier and more successful as teenagers than those who opted for the 'marshmallow in the hand'. When it came to university entrance, the children who had held out (at four years old) performed considerably better in the US entrance tests – a fact that would not have been predicted by their IQs.

Delayed gratification crops up repeatedly in descriptions of emotional intelligence. It is a factor that constantly recurs throughout life, whether studying and sacrificing for an academic or career goal, overcoming business obstacles for longer-term profits, or arduous training and social sacrifices in attaining a sporting accolade. In short, it is part of the wider definition of intelligence we have already met.

A person displaying this intelligence factor doesn't have to have everything 'right now'. In an age of instant products and services many have lost the art of patience, and the willingness to trade-off present pains for disproportionately greater pleasure in the future. We don't need to look far for examples of colleagues and friends who lack impulse control. It fuels violence, crime, broken relationships and much human misery. It is a learnt trait, however. Most children in due course learn to wait, and delaying gratification becomes a habit. We instinctively work out acceptable trade-offs – a 'bird in the hand, or two in the bush' – in all sorts of day-to-day decisions. It is a peculiarly human trait, unknown amongst the lower animals. That fact alone points to its importance as a feature of intelligence.

Impulse control, as illustrated so elegantly by four-year-olds in the marshmallow test, is a master skill and illustrates the sophistication of human intelligence. It is a triumph of the reasoning brain over the impulsive one, yet never shows up on an IQ test.

Managing moods

Emotional competence includes the capacity to stay calm, to shake off anxiety, gloom, or irritability. It means not being *at the mercy* of emotion. People who are poor in this emotional competence are constantly battling feelings of anxiety and regret. Those who excel in it can bounce back far more quickly from life's setbacks. Handling feelings is an ability that follows naturally from knowing our feelings. Self-awareness, in turn, is a key trait of emotional intelligence.

Expressing and repressing emotions

Managing emotions doesn't mean repressing feelings. That has got psychoanalysts rich but isn't a good example of intelligence. Aristotle wrote 'Anyone can become angry – that is easy. But to be angry with the right person, to the right degree, at the right time, for the right purpose, and in the right way – that is not easy'. Nor does managing emotions necessarily mean expressing them. 'Wearing your heart on your sleeve', for instance, although laudable in some individual cases, might not display emotional intelligence. Conversely, and again in different situations, harbouring bitter, harmful emotions can be foolish in the extreme.

Feelings can be managed in different ways. Some people recommend expressing anger to get it out of the system. Experimental evidence, however, seems to indicate that giving vent to anger produces more anger. Relaxation skills, meditation, deep breathing – or just counting to ten – can be a more effective, intelligent emotional response. In either case, emotion makes more sense as a servant than a master.

Some emotional responses are ephemeral, however intense. Others become fully paid-up habits and affect our general motivation and mood. Moods can be positive or negative, of course. Positive or empowering moods contribute to a feeling of well-being. Disempowering moods and lack of motivation have an equivalent harmful effect on us. Moods can help or hinder us in getting what we want. They may be suitable or unsuitable in different situations and contexts. There is sometimes a time to be angry, for instance, and there may be a place for fear or hate.

There are no marks just for being an emotional animal, or even in emotional expression, in which three-years-olds display such virtuosity. The *intelligence* is in understanding, managing and controlling these primeval, indispensable features of our humanity.

Popular EQ definitions often include specific emotions. In particular, personality traits such as 'optimism', 'persistence' and 'warmth' are quoted. So EQ finishes up as comprising everything that IQ is not, which is an awful lot. Mayer, for instance, doesn't see *positive* emotions as being essential. He says, for instance, that a person can be depressed (part of the human condition from time to time) and yet have a high emotional intelligence. He or she might well identify a reason for their condition, and, through better self knowledge and cognition, be more likely to climb out of their condition given time. This is where knowing what you want is important, as we saw in Chapter 3. We apply our intelligence to a purpose, and whatever helps us to achieve that purpose – including 'negative' emotions (although emotions are often in the eye of the beholder) – supports and enhances that intelligence.

Motivating yourself

Marshalling emotions in the service of a goal is essential for paying attention, for self-motivation and mastery, and for creativity. Emotional self-control often means delaying gratification and stifling impulsiveness, and underlies accomplishments of every sort. It may determine whether you have the motivation to see a task through to a successful conclusion. More positively, being able to get into the 'flow' state enables outstanding performance of all kinds. People who have this skill tend to be highly productive and effective in whatever they undertake. These first three emotional intelligence domains correspond to intrapersonal intelligence we discussed above.

Mood management self-assessment

Answer these simple questions to help you assess your mood-management intelligence:

- Can you easily reframe or re-vision a painful experience?
- Can you handle rejection?
- Do you generally look on the brighter side of life?
- Do you manage adversity well?
- Would others describe you as a positive person?
- Can you see the 'silver lining' in most clouds?
- Are you generally satisfied with your life?

- Would you say you are happy?
- Do you enjoy yourself and other people?
- Are you having wholesome fun in life right now?
- Can you easily express positive feelings?
- Would others describe you as a person with lots of drive?

Mood management does not lend itself to IQ-type scoring. There aren't even right and wrong answers. Emotional intelligence applies in a context, and within a purpose. Part of 'intelligence' is to act appropriately in that context, and in pursuing that purpose. Nor can handling emotions truly be isolated as a single factor of emotional intelligence. Some people handle anger well, but can't handle fear. Some people can't experience real joy, and so on. Each emotion therefore has to be judged and managed differently, from person to person and from situation to situation. The upside of this is that we can identify and manage emotions *one at a time* and thus improve our emotional intelligence in an incremental, but over a period, significant way.

There is no one-time eleven-plus-type life-significant test of emotional intelligence. Just as when learning a skill like driving a car, we can only take in one or two things at once. We learn best incrementally, so it would be a formidable task to boost our mood management skills – let alone overall emotional intelligence – as a single project. The project carries on as you read and think.

EQ in business

Just as Gardner's multiple intelligences have taken a strong foothold in education, especially in the USA, EQ is proving to be a saleable product to business and the workplace. People skills, we know, are all-important within organizations and teams. They also figure high in evergreen topics such as leadership and human resources management. So it is no surprise that emotional intelligence has been welcomed as an approach to doing what empowerment, re-engineering and decades of management panaceas have failed to do.

Different studies have found that the most valued and productive staff are those who display emotional intelligence, and don't necessarily have a high IQ. This includes engineers, accountants and various professions as well as salespeople, managers and the sort of people usually associated with 'people' jobs. Lack of emotional intelligence explains why, not only do people of high IQ often land up in lower job functions (working for less 'intelligent' people), but why they can be such disastrous pilots of their personal lives.

There are, of course, some job areas where analytical, intellectual, cognitive abilities will get you a long way. But those situations are fewer than we might imagine. Moreover, computers increasingly tackle complex but logical, programmable processes, so we are less reliant on that kind of human intelligence. In any event, 'left-brain' skills are not enough in the top, leadership positions. The real problems of business invariably involve people rather than machines, and emotions rather than logic and cool rationale. So EQ – which, as we have seen, is readily learnable – is a powerful management development tool that will take a manager much further than IQ-type knowledge.

It is hard to think of organizational and management problems that do not require some of the characteristics of emotional intelligence we have met. Consider the following situation. You have to hire some new employees for your rapidly expanding business. You know that some of your staff are not pulling their weight. When you hired these people, they came with what you thought were the right qualifications, but you have come to realize that they only had skills in the technical, task-related routines they were trained in. You now know that their interpersonal and team skills and general initiative are missing. You are determined not to let that happen again.

If you could do it all over again, what criteria would you use to hire people with the all-round skills you require, assuming their technical skills reached the necessary level. Would you choose people who:

- are able to interact well with people, are team players, are responsible and dependable, have good social skills and relate well to others?
- can cope with work demands, effectively 'size up' and deal with problem situations, are generally flexible, realistic, effective in understanding these problem situations and competent at solving them?
- can deal with stress without 'falling apart' or losing control, are generally calm, rarely impulsive, and work well under pressure?
- enjoy life, have an optimistic, cheerful, hopeful outlook and create a healthy positive motivational work environment?

When cases such as this one are addressed in terms of intelligence factors of the kinds we have discussed, and specific intra- and interpersonal skills, the solution becomes all but obvious. Emotional intelligence is important, not just because it reflects true intelligence, but because it can be translated into practical benefits in a way that does not apply to a narrower measure of 'brainpower'. EQ is *common sense*, which may be none too common, but, as we have seen, is nonetheless learnable and well within the potential of each of us.

Try an EQ test

There are no EQ (or EIQ) validated tests as is the case with IQ tests. The tests that do exist, and the ideas on which they are based, have proliferated over the Internet and vary enormously in both scope and quality. Most are in the 'fun' category, although many are clothed in seemingly reputable academic or professional garb. Many are a marketing front for a book, consultancy or training.

EQ scores do not affect us in our education and careers as may be the case with IQ. Even if of value, they are not recognized by employers or academic organizations. So EQ scores are not an issue. However, the tests themselves illustrate, in a lot of detail, the many factors upon which emotional intelligence is based that we have covered in this chapter. Moreover, doing tests is a way to increase your awareness or self-knowledge, which we saw was an important aspect of intrapersonal intelligence.

Test yourself

You can do the following test online at *www.queendom.com*. The analysis of your answers is not included in this book, but you can fill it out here first so that you can submit it more quickly. There is no time limit. The assessment software is also available for downloading and you can find out more about this from the site. The author is grateful to Ilona Jerabek who compiled the test, and Plumeus Inc for permission to reproduce it here as one of the better examples of currently available EQ psychometric tests.

In order to obtain valid results, you need to answer all the questions. Read every statement carefully and indicate which option applies best to you. There may be some questions describing situations that do not apply to you. In such cases, select an answer which would be most likely if you ever found yourself in such a situation. Before you submit your test for scoring, make sure you have answered all the questions.

1. When I feel awful, I don't know what or who is upsetting me.

a) most of the time
b) often
c) sometimes
d) rarely
e) almost never

2. Even when I do my best, I feel guilty about the things that did not get done.
   a) most of the time
   b) often
   c) sometimes
   d) rarely
   e) almost never

3. Everybody has some problem, but there are so many things wrong with me that I simply cannot like myself.
   a) most of the time
   b) often
   c) sometimes
   d) rarely
   e) almost never

4. When I am upset, I can pinpoint exactly what aspect of the problem bugs me.
   a) most of the time
   b) often
   c) sometimes
   d) rarely
   e) almost never

5. Some people make me feel bad about myself, no matter what I do.
   a) strongly agree
   b) agree
   c) partially agree/disagree
   d) disagree
   e) strongly disagree

6. I buy things that I can't really afford.
   a) regularly
   b) often
   c) sometimes
   d) rarely
   e) almost never

7. When I mess up, I say self-depreciating things, such as 'I am such a loser,' 'Stupid, stupid, stupid,' or 'I can't do anything right.'
   a) most of the time
   b) often
   c) sometimes
   d) rarely
   e) almost never

8. I am ashamed about how I look or behave.
   a) most of the time
   b) often
   c) sometimes
   d) rarely
   e) almost never

9. I feel uneasy in situations where I am expected to display affection.
   a) most of the time
   b) often
   c) sometimes
   d) rarely
   e) almost never

10. I feel weird when I hug someone other than my close family.
    a) very true
    b) mostly true
    c) somewhat true

d) mostly not true
e) not true at all

11. When I see something that I like or want, I can't get it out of my head until I get it.
    a) very true
    b) mostly true
    c) somewhat true
    d) mostly not true
    e) not true at all

12. Although there might be things to improve, I like myself the way I am.
    a) strongly agree
    b) agree
    c) partially agree/disagree
    d) disagree
    e) strongly disagree

13. I say things that I later regret.
    a) regularly
    b) often
    c) sometimes
    d) rarely
    e) almost never

14. I get into a mode where I feel strong, capable and competent.
    a) regularly
    b) often
    c) sometimes
    d) rarely
    e) almost never

15. I panic when I have to face someone who is angry.
    a) most of the time

b) often
c) sometimes
d) rarely
e) almost never

16. I am under the impression that people's reactions come out of the blue.
    a) most of the time
    b) often
    c) sometimes
    d) rarely
    e) almost never

17. I have a need to make a difference.
    a) very true
    b) mostly true
    c) somewhat true
    d) mostly not true
    e) not true at all

18. I cannot get over the guilt that I feel because of trivial mistakes and faux pas that I made in the past.
    a) very true
    b) mostly true
    c) somewhat true
    d) mostly not true
    e) not true at all

19. When I resolve to achieve something, I run into obstacles that keep me from reaching my goals.
    a) regularly
    b) often
    c) sometimes
    d) rarely
    e) almost never

20. I cannot stop thinking about my problems.
    a) most of the time
    b) often
    c) sometimes
    d) rarely
    e) almost never

21. It is better to remain cold and neutral until you really get to know a person.
    a) strongly agree
    b) agree
    c) partially agree/disagree
    d) disagree
    e) strongly disagree

22. I will do whatever I can to keep myself from crying.
    a) most of the time
    b) often
    c) sometimes
    d) rarely
    e) almost never

23. I have difficulty saying things like 'I love you,' even when I really feel them.
    a) most of the time
    b) often
    c) sometimes
    d) rarely
    e) almost never

24. I enjoy spending time with my friend(s).
    a) most of the time
    b) often
    c) sometimes
    d) rarely
    e) almost never

25. I do my best even if there is nobody to see it.
    a) most of the time
    b) often
    c) sometimes
    d) rarely
    e) almost never

26. I am bored.
    a) most of the time
    b) often
    c) sometimes
    d) rarely
    e) almost never

27. I pay people compliments when they deserve them.
    a) most of the time
    b) often
    c) sometimes
    d) rarely
    e) almost never

28. I worry about things that other people don't even think about.
    a) most of the time
    b) often
    c) sometimes
    d) rarely
    e) almost never

29. I need someone's push in order to get going.
    a) most of the time
    b) often
    c) sometimes
    d) rarely
    e) almost never

30. People who are emotional make me uncomfortable.
    a) very true
    b) mostly true
    c) somewhat true
    d) mostly not true
    e) not true at all

31. When someone does me a favour without being asked, I wonder what his/her real agenda is.
    a) very true
    b) mostly true
    c) somewhat true
    d) mostly not true
    e) not true at all

32. My life is full of dead ends.
    a) very true
    b) mostly true
    c) somewhat true
    d) mostly not true
    e) not true at all

33. I am not satisfied with my work unless someone else praises it.
    a) very true
    b) mostly true
    c) somewhat true
    d) mostly not true
    e) not true at all

34. When I hear about someone's problem, several possible solutions immediately pop up in my head.
    a) most of the time
    b) often
    c) sometimes
    d) rarely
    e) almost never

35. I do what people expect me to, even when I disagree with them.
    a) most of the time
    b) often
    c) sometimes
    d) rarely
    e) almost never

36. People tell me that I overreact to minor problems.
    a) regularly
    b) often
    c) sometimes
    d) rarely
    e) almost never

37. I finish what I set out to do.
    a) most of the time
    b) often
    c) sometimes
    d) rarely
    e) almost never

38. No matter how much I accomplish, I have a nagging feeling that I should be doing more.
    a) most of the time
    b) often
    c) sometimes
    d) rarely
    e) almost never

39. I am unhappy for reasons I can't understand.
    a) very true
    b) mostly true
    c) somewhat true
    d) mostly not true
    e) not true at all

40. I have ____________ confidence in my abilities.
    a) complete
    b) a lot of
    c) some
    d) little
    e) no

41. I feel ____________ deviating from standard procedures/strategies.
    a) incapable of
    b) very uncomfortable
    c) quite uncomfortable
    d) somewhat uncomfortable
    e) comfortable
    f) very comfortable

42. When I fail at a task or do worse than I would like to, it is usually due to ____________
    a) lack of preparation or effort on my part
    b) lack of concentration or attention on my part
    c) lack of ability on my part
    d) external factors, ie things that have nothing to do with me, such as an unreasonably difficult task, bad weather/timing
    e) internal factors (ie my traits and characteristics, such as IQ, talents etc) beyond my control
    f) a combination of factors, mostly things that I can change
    g) a combination of factors, mostly things that I can't change

43. I open up and talk about my most intimate issues and private feelings with anybody, anytime, in any circumstances.
    a) exactly – I am willing and able to share and discuss anything with anybody, no matter the time and place

b) it depends – I share and discuss my intimate issues with some people, but there are circumstances where it can be a mistake or inappropriate
c) it depends – I share and discuss my intimate issues with some people, but in most circumstances, it can be a mistake or inappropriate
d) no way – intimate issues should not be discussed with anybody except for the closest family members or friends
e) no way – people should deal with intimate issues by themselves

44. I get most motivated when I ____________
a) picture the worst possible outcome and then do my best to avoid it
b) picture the best possible outcome and then do my best to achieve it
c) picture the expected outcome and then do my best to achieve it
d) picture the acceptable outcome and then do my best to achieve it
e) forget the possible outcome and just do what needs to be done

45. Sizing up people's character is ____________
a) one of my strongest points
b) something I am relatively good at
c) something I am not very good at
d) one of my weakest points
e) something that I don't bother doing
f) something that doesn't interest me at all
g) something that I never attempt

46. When there is something unpleasant to do, I ________
a) do it right away and get it over with
b) postpone it until I feel like doing it

c) postpone it until I have nothing else to do
d) postpone it until it is too late and it gets dropped
e) wait until I have no other choice but to do it
f) find a way to reward myself for doing it and then do it
g) break the task into small steps and do them one by one
h) find an acceptable valid reason why I cannot do the task and get rid of it
i) find someone else to do it for me

47. In my view, happiness depends mostly on __________
a) society and economy
b) one's background
c) the way one was treated as a child
d) one's environment
e) the people one is surrounded by
f) the way one leads his/her life
g) one's luck

48. When I am upset, I ___________
a) can tell exactly how I feel, (ie whether I feel sad, betrayed, lonely, annoyed, angry, etc)
b) can usually tell how I feel (ie whether I feel sad, betrayed, lonely, annoyed, angry, etc), but sometimes it is difficult to distinguish what exactly I am feeling
c) usually cannot distinguish what exactly I am feeling
d) don't lose time trying to figure out what exactly I am feeling

49. In my social group (workplace, school, neighbourhood, community, extended family, etc), ____________ who likes whom, who cannot stand whom, who has a crush on whom, etc.

a) I am always well aware of
b) I am usually well aware of
c) I don't pay any attention to
d) I don't pay much attention to
e) I sometimes notice
f) I cannot figure out

50. When I have a major problem that I find extremely difficult to deal with, I ____________
a) will deal with it by myself
b) go to family members for advice and/or support
c) go to my friend(s) for advice and/or support
d) go to my therapist/counsellor for advice and/or support
e) try to distract myself
f) submerge myself in unrelated work
g) try to forget about it
h) will pretend it does not exist

51. When I am upset (for example, after dealing with a difficult person), I ____________
a) step back and reassess the situation
b) take it out on someone
c) step back and find a way to calm down
d) find a reason to blow out
e) step back and console myself
f) find it difficult to calm down
g) start doing things that I later regret
h) talk to someone to get it off my chest

52. When people make important decisions, they use different strategies and pay attention to different aspects of the situation. In your case, what impact does your gut feeling have on your decision? How I feel about the possible outcomes has ____________
a) absolutely no bearing on the decision

b) very little bearing on the decision
c) some bearing on the decision
d) considerable bearing on the decision
e) a lot of bearing on the decision

53. When someone snaps at me, ____________
   a) I quickly retaliate
   b) I panic
   c) I withdraw feeling hurt
   d) I ask for an explanation
   e) I get very upset
   f) I get very angry
   g) I am hurt and start crying
   h) I let it go without confronting the person
   i) I ignore it
   j) I confront the person

54. When a new prospect comes along, ____________
   a) I remain sceptical until I have reasons to change my attitude
   b) I don't expect much; that way, I never get disappointed
   c) I have no preconceptions and take it as it comes
   d) I expect the best; if it does not work out, I will deal with it

55. When I break a rule (without breaking the law), _____
   a) I feel bad for a long time
   b) I feel bad for quite a bit of time and then get over it
   c) I feel bad but get over it relatively quickly
   d) I don't allow myself to feel bad
   e) I don't really care

56. People differ greatly in how much importance friendships carry for them. Having said that, which of the statements below describes you best?

a) I make acquaintances and friends easily
b) I make acquaintances easily but it takes some time to make a really good friend
c) I make acquaintances with some difficulty and it takes even more time to make a really good friend
d) I remain mistrustful for a long time before I allow someone in
e) It is difficult for me to make new friends and acquaintances
f) I am unable to make acquaintances or friends

57. When I get frustrated, ____________
a) I almost always drop what I am doing and go and use my time more productively
b) I usually drop what I am doing and go and use my time more productively
c) I sometimes drop what I am doing and go and use my time more productively
d) I sometimes persist and finish the task
e) I usually persist and finish the task
f) I almost always persist and finish the task
g) I take a break and then continue the task

58. When I need to communicate my positive feelings to someone, I prefer to ____________
a) act it out by doing something nice for the person
b) say it to the person
c) write it to the person
d) tell it to someone else, hoping that the message will get to the right person
e) keep it to myself in order not to spoil the person
f) keep it to myself and hope that the person will notice what a good mood I am in
g) keep it to myself; if he/she really loves/likes me, he/she will know how I feel

59. What is the best timing for revealing shocking news (coming out of the closet, announcing a divorce, admitting infidelity, etc) to one's family?
    a) when the family enters a transition phase (relocating, changing jobs, divorce, etc), killing two birds with one stone
    b) at weddings, funerals, religious holidays, etc, when most family members are present
    c) when the family is doing generally fine or during a quiet period
    d) when the family learns about another shocker, killing two birds with one stone
    e) immediately or as soon as possible, regardless of other circumstances

60. In general, it is best ____________
    a) not to set goals at all and just go with the flow
    b) to set goals that are a piece of cake
    c) to set goals that are relatively easy to achieve and not too challenging
    d) to set goals that are challenging but possible to achieve
    e) to set goals that are so challenging that they are very difficult to achieve
    f) to set goals way above one's capability

61. Emma is a self-made entrepreneur. Despite her limited education, she is able to successfully run her small business – a bed and breakfast with a gift shop. She is a great mother and is well liked in the community. When Emma goes to a party or another social gathering, she avoids talking about anything except for her children, b & b in America and local events. The reason for her to be annoyed about any other topic is:
    a) her belief in the future of bed and breakfast in the United States

b) her belief that children are the most fascinating subject
c) her belief that everybody would find these topics fascinating
d) her wish to keep the conversation within neutral limits
e) her wish to keep the conversation within limits of her expertise
f) her wish to avoid hot topics, such as politics, abortion or capital punishment

62. Tony, aged 39, has been battling his weight problem for most of his teen and adult life. He has tried numerous diets, used various weight-loss pills and started many short-lived exercise programmes. Nothing has ever worked, in part because he was never able to stick with the weight-loss programme. Next month, he will turn 40 and he decided that this millstone will mark the end of his chubby days – he is going to lose weight and stay trim, no matter what it takes. He is highly motivated, ready to starve until his last fat cell runs dry. Which weight-loss strategy would give him the best chance of reaching his goal?
    a) save some money and go for liposuction; he won't be able to lose weight otherwise
    b) begin an extremely easy programme (substituting certain items with low fat/low calories equivalents) that will require little willpower and will yield first results after several weeks
    c) begin a regular diet that will yield a loss of a few pounds within the first two weeks and leave exercising alone since he hates it anyway
    d) begin a regular diet that will yield a loss of a few pounds within the first two weeks and combine it with light exercise

e) begin a crash diet that will yield a loss of several pounds within days and leave exercising alone, since he hates it anyway
f) begin an extremely difficult programme (crash diet plus heavy exercise) that will require a lot of willpower and will yield first results within days

63. Nancy is a very capable secretary, but she has a difficult personality. She works at a medical school for a professor. She is usually nice with her superiors, but she sticks strictly to her job description. She cannot get along with any of the other secretaries; in fact, she behaves as if she were superior to them. She gives an especially hard time to all the students. She keeps them waiting needlessly, snaps at them, dwells on their minor mistakes, and truly enjoys when they get in trouble. The reason for Nancy's behaviour toward the students is:
a) that she has an inferiority complex and compensates this way
b) that she wishes she could stay longer in school and resents all those who do
c) that she believes that all the students are incompetent
d) that she has had a bad experience with students and prefers to keep them at a safe distance
e) that she has low opinion about the quality of today's higher education system
f) that she is jealous of the students
g) that she is a sick, irrational and unpredictable person
h) that she is introverted and prefers to be alone
i) that she in fact believes herself to be smarter than everybody else is

64. (Background is in previous question) For you as a new student, the best way to get along with Nancy is to:
   a) become friends with her
   b) show her how smart you really are
   c) ignore her completely (avoid greeting her, small talk, etc)
   d) remind her in a friendly manner what her job and place is
   e) treat her with respect without becoming too chummy
   f) show her that you admire her expertise as a secretary and ask her for advice
   g) give her a taste of her own medicine
   h) ask her why she is so nasty while all the other secretaries are so nice and helpful
   i) show her compassion and tell her that not everybody can get into medical school
   j) tell her to seek professional help for her emotional problems
   k) engage her in a discussion about her views of education
   l) tell her that she is not smarter than everybody; if she were, she would not be behaving this way

65. You have an opportunity to work on an important project that could secure your professional career. However, there is a contest and a committee composed of five members will choose the best proposal. You have spent a lot of time and effort preparing the proposal, and you are quite proud of the results. Unfortunately, you come in third. What do you do?
   a) get the winner's proposal and try to figure out in what aspect it was better than yours
   b) confront the committee members and explain to them how they hurt you by not choosing your proposal

c) confront the committee members and let them know what a mistake they made by passing on your proposal
d) persuade yourself that it was not such a big deal and it was hardly worth the effort
e) realize that you are really a loser and will never amount to anything
f) find reasons to believe that there was a conflict of interest and the selection was not fair
g) shake the defeat off and go on with life

66. You are single and your last date turned out to be someone totally incompatible, again. You look back and realize that you haven't had a decent date for two years. How do you react?
a) remain optimistic and decide to keep dating until you find the right person
b) decide to give up dating forever, and concentrate on more worthwhile things
c) decide to stop dating for now and wait for the right person to find you
d) decide to go out with people who are somehow different from your typical dates
e) decide to have a look and figure out why you have been falling for the wrong people
f) decide to stick with the next one and invest in changing the person into who you want him/her to be
g) decide to lower your standards because, apparently, this is as good as it gets

67. Your best friend's grandmother died a month ago. They were very close and your friend is devastated. It is best ____________
a) to leave your friend alone and not to disturb him/her

b) to take your friend out dancing
c) to take your friend out to see a comedy
d) to take your friend out to see a drama about losing someone close
e) to encourage him/her to cry it out
f) to encourage him/her to toughen up
g) to tell him/her to get over it; life goes on
h) to tell him/her about your own problems to take their mind off his/her grief
i) to hang around and be available
j) to follow your friend's lead in whatever he/she wants to do

68. Speaking out about negative emotions is ___________
a) always unhealthy, regardless of circumstances
b) generally unhealthy but necessary in some circumstances
c) healthy for some people, unhealthy for others
d) generally healthy but inappropriate in some circumstances
e) always healthy, regardless of circumstances

69. You are in the middle of a heated argument with your spouse/boyfriend/girlfriend/friend. Although you normally like this person, you are so furious that you are about to say something very nasty, something that you know will hurt him/her. The best way to deal with this kind of situation is to ___________
a) say that you are too angry and set a different time to continue the argument
b) say whatever is on your mind; he/she needs to know how you feel and deal with it
c) say whatever is on your mind, live through the storm and look forward to the make-up
d) start crying
e) just walk away

f) walk away saying that you don't want to talk about it anymore
g) give yourself time-out and continue after having calmed down
h) swallow your anger and continue the argument
i) let the anger out because it is unhealthy to bottle up emotions
j) let the anger out and apologize later on
k) proclaim that you refuse to have a battle of wits with an unarmed person and walk away

70. You are part of a group that has been working together for two hours, trying to solve a difficult and pressing problem that calls for a creative approach. Everybody is getting tired and edgy. Basically, you are stuck. The best way to go about it is to ___________
a) tell a joke, or find another way to make people laugh
b) go through solutions to past problems in search for inspiration
c) apply pressure on the group, telling them that this is not a joke – they'd better figure out something, and fast!
d) initiate brainstorming
e) take turns in making suggestions
f) to motivate the group, review the importance of finding a solution.

6

Thinking like a genius

There is no practical limit to human intelligence. Nor is there a limit, given a normal brain, to the potential intelligence of an individual person. This should come as no surprise. It is a well-established fact that we never use our minds to their full potential. One of the interesting discoveries from neuroscience is that we can create new neural connections up to any age *just by thinking*. That means more brainpower, more true learning, and more intelligence. We always have spare capacity for a few more billion neural connections. We can all 'grow' our brains in this way, regardless of our genetic inheritance and whatever limiting self-beliefs we have picked up from childhood.

In this chapter you will learn how to increase your intelligence to a significantly higher level. This is based on what you have learnt so far. Everything still applies – you can't shortcut the ABCs of emotional intelligence. On that foundation, you can then apply further tips and techniques based on characteristics that have come to be associated with high intelligence, or genius. In particular, you can focus on one or more specific types of intelligence we have covered that particularly appeal to you. If you want to raise your intelligence sights, use this chapter as an intelligence masterclass.

By following the principles and techniques you have met so far, you can dramatically increase your true intelligence, depending on your starting level and your willingness to change. Change may occur in different areas of your life, and in the different kinds of intelligence we have met. The degree to which a person will improve in different types of intelligence will vary a lot. Some aspects of intelligence may be latent, having been suppressed by adverse environmental, educational and self-image factors. We all experience these negative factors to some degree, and part of emotional intelligence is to ride these hurdles without undue adverse effect. However, such latent talents or half-forgotten childhood dreams can bloom very quickly with the right sort of nurture, resulting in extraordinary life changes. For all practical purposes, however, the bottom line is simple: you can set your sights as high as you like, from any starting point.

Making an intelligent choice

In Chapter 1 you met a range of 'intelligences'. These help us to appreciate aspects of our intelligence we may not have recognized, and to which we have given little attention. Once you can identify the sort of mental resources that you can call upon, you can choose the type of intelligence in which you want to excel and the level to which you want to aspire.

Where do I start?

We each start from a different level in our quest for excellence. If you are starting off from a position of already 'high' (albeit unmeasured) intelligence, of whatever kind, the improvement may not be dramatic. That is because the law of diminishing returns begins to take effect, in which you require a lot of effort for a small improvement. Just like an athlete trying to knock that extra fraction of a second off his sprint time, a lot of hard work and dedication may be required before you reach the next critical level of competence. Put simply, the going gets harder nearer the top. However, as with the athlete, there is always room for improvement. Moreover, as with Roger Bannister's historical, record-breaking four-minute mile in the 1950s, the barrier may well be psychological. Success depends as much on self-beliefs and state of mind as hereditary gifts. The breakthrough to any true mastery often boils down to mental factors: self-image, self-motivation, the strength of a dream, a clearly visualized goal. In short, human excellence is built on the foundation of intrapersonal intelligence; it starts inside.

If you are starting from an average level – let's say that you are reasonably competent when it comes to people skills – you can expect a far greater relative improvement. This is akin to acquiring athletic competence from a lower level of fitness, experience and know-how. In such cases you will have plenty of scope for improvement before the law of diminishing returns sets in.

However, you can expect even bigger relative improvements in any area of your life where you are below par. If at the level 'I'm hopeless at remembering people's names', for instance, you can expect a massive increase in that specific kind of intelligence once you apply yourself to it, and seek out the appropriate know-how. You may have identified the areas in which you want to improve as you carried out the SMART goal-setting process in Chapter 3 as part of your intrapersonal intelligence programme. Otherwise, you just need to make your 'intelligence' choice, and decide in which area you would like to be brilliant.

Setting your mind

After following the goal-setting process in Chapter 3, self-motivation comes built-in with your SMART choice of goal. That is, you are *automatically* drawn towards a *compelling goal*. That's what helps you to get started, keep going, and finally achieve what you set out to achieve. You don't need special psyching up. Just do the common sense goal-setting exercises and follow the process. Set your mind on a goal, including the goal of becoming more intelligent. You will then discover sources of knowledge, ways of learning, and skills you can acquire along the way. For instance, you can draw on books, friends, the Internet, night school courses and so on. This author has published a book entitled *Remembering Names and Faces* that will bring remarkable improvements in that specific area. But there is plenty of learning material available on a whole range of mind-improving topics. To be intelligent means to take responsibility for your learning and personal development. High intelligence reveals itself in statements like 'I don't know, but I'll find out' and 'I'll give it a try'.

It's up to you which aspects of your intelligence you want to develop to a level of mastery (or genius, if you like). In most cases we have so much latent skill and unused brain capacity that more or less anything is possible. We just need to be motivated to improve, and to be open to learning and change. You can seek to improve or excel in existing competencies, correct intelligence blind spots, or simply widen and develop your whole personal repertoire of intelligences. Your choice will depend on what's important to you right now, including the importance you give to the different aspects of intelligence we have met.

Your desire for mastery may involve unfulfilled childhood dreams, opportunities missed, or the buzz of a new challenge. Your 'intelligent intelligence choice' may also depend on what will presently be of most use in your job, family life, and hobbies – the extent to which you can *apply* your newly-released brainpower. In some areas, depending on your circumstances and starting point, a small improvement, requiring little time and effort, might bring disproportionately high benefits. A characteristic of mastery is to take the easiest, most pleasurable route, so you need not feel guilty.

By honing the intrapersonal, self-awareness skills you met in Chapter 3, you will be able to get the right balance between your goals and values, and the resources you need to achieve them. From what you learn in the rest of this chapter, you can be more selective and bring about extraordinary change in chosen areas of your life.

The secrets of super intelligence

Improving certain characteristics of intelligence enables us to 'achieve' to a level well above normal. High achievement usually demands a certain level of overall intelligence – especially emotional intelligence. As we have seen, EQ converts readily into success in career and personal life. These special characteristics are usually associated with 'very successful people', leaders, top managers, great artists and scientists. Sometimes they are linked to mastery, or genius.

Amazingly, even at this level, there is no exclusive, genetically blessed group of humans. In fact, some of the common features of such outstanding people are well known, and just as learnable as the common-sense principles and techniques you have learnt so far. There is certainly no evidence that the geniuses of the world (or members of MENSA, the high IQ club) have bigger than average brains. Nor do they usually boast an impressive, intellectual family pedigree. If you did happen to choose the right parents, that's a bonus. The difference at this level is more to do with self-belief, creativity, dedication, 'vision' and a strong self-image. In other words, with the intrapersonal aspects of intelligence we have already met.

Historically, the sorts of 'super intelligence' characteristics you will meet in this chapter have been associated with hereditary 'gifts' and talents, or even some mystical human quality, rather than more common manifestations of human attainment. More recently, neuroscience has revealed more and more of the awesome potential of the normal brain. Mystique is starting to give way to common sense, learnable, *do-able* traits and skills that *any* brain can attain to.

The so-called traits of genius are no better defined and validated than intelligence itself. However, they offer simple, common-sense methods for qualitative improvements in the different types of intelligence we have discussed so far. Importantly, an understanding of these characteristics brings higher levels of intelligence within the practical reach of otherwise very average people.

The starting point is quite basic: look at these special, yet simple intelligence characteristics as being within your potential. That is, as being possible. Initially this entails no more than exploring and exploiting the potential of your mind. Some of the exercises in goal setting and identifying values in Chapter 3 involved just such self-knowledge. It may mean having to stretch yourself mentally, just as you would need to stretch your body through exercises over a period to reach a peak of fitness. More than anything, aspiring to loftier levels of intelligence means trusting your awesome brainpower, and letting your unconscious mind do what it alone is capable of doing.

Thankfully, unlike serious physical training, mental fitness can mean gain without pain, once you understand the principles and acquire the know-how. Your brain doesn't hurt when you use it in the right way. And the benefits go well beyond those of physical prowess. Change at deep levels of the mind cannot but affect all your behaviour, and every part of your life. The control centre of your mind is where it all happens. We are what we think. The effects of intelligence are all pervading, and the benefits may be greater than you ever could have imagined.

Modelling mastery

We can start by observing, and then copying, or 'modelling', people who exhibit special intelligence. For instance, how do geniuses come up with ideas? What is common to the thinking style that produced the Mona Lisa, the discovery of penicillin, the theory of relativity, the invention of the Walkman, or Velcro? What characterizes the thinking strategies of the Einsteins, Edisons, da Vincis, Darwins, Picassos, Michelangelos, Galileos, Freuds and Mozarts of history? What can we learn from them?

For years, scholars and researchers tried to study genius by analysing statistics, as if piles of data somehow would reveal its secrets. One study at the beginning of the twentieth century found that most geniuses are fathered by men older than 30, had mothers younger than 25, and usually were sickly as children. Other scholars reported that many were celibate (Descartes); others were fatherless (Dickens) or motherless (Darwin). In the end, the piles of data illuminated nothing for the would-be genius to actually emulate.

The subject is critical to education, and over the years academics have tried to find the links between normal intelligence and genius. But, as with the IQ movement, which we discussed in the first chapter, a narrow, intellectual definition of intelligence was used. Repeatedly, when it comes to outstanding achievement, it turns out that academic intelligence is not enough. For instance, run-of-the-mill scientists have IQs much higher than acclaimed geniuses. Nobel prizewinner Richard Feynman, for example, widely acclaimed for his extraordinary genius, weighs in at a not-very-earth-shattering IQ of 122. Disparity of this sort is widespread and further confirms the wider nature of true intelligence.

Genius is not about scoring 1600 on the SAT, mastering a dozen languages just for fun, finishing MENSA exercises in record time, having an extraordinarily high IQ, or even being 'smart'. Rather, EQ and other aspects of our multiple intelligences seem to crop up more frequently when researching genius. Creativity, for instance, conspicuously absent from any IQ-type definition of intelligence, is often correlated with outstanding achievers. After considerable debate initiated in the 1960s by psychologist Joy P. Guilford, psychologists concluded that creativity is not the same as intelligence. An individual (so they maintained) can be far more creative than intelligent, or far more intelligent than creative. Interestingly, creativity as such does not figure in Goleman's EQ critical characteristics list, although it gets a mention as one of Gardner's multiple intelligences. However, it takes on special significance when addressing very high intelligence, outstanding achievement, and the idea of genius.

Features of high intelligence

So what are the features of high intelligence: giftedness, genius, and outstanding people? More specifically for our purposes, what features might the average brain owner emulate (or just check out) to his or her advantage? In fact, many such features have been identified. Some are general and others are quite specific. Each has different relevance from person to person (eg in their work), and mostly features in the different types of intelligences we have met. But, importantly, each characteristic is, to some degree, *learnable*. That means that we can all be not just more intelligent, but attain, in one or more areas of our life, very high levels of 'true' intelligence.

In the rest of this chapter, some of the features associated with high intelligence and special human achievement will be described:

- put your thoughts into pictures;
- make novel combinations;

- sleep on it;
- go for quantity;
- expect the unexpected;
- change your perspective;
- create ambivalence;
- model your own creativity;
- think metaphorically;
- take an interest;
- create chances;
- change;
- think laterally.

Put your thoughts into pictures

One characteristic of genius is thinking *visually*. Vision, of course, is the dominant sense, and we don't get far – internally or externally – without it. Put your thoughts into pictures. When internally setting your goals (Chapter 3), clearly imagine the successful outcome, as vividly as possible. When considering a problem, see each aspect of it, or different scenarios. The more sensory, or realistic your internal model of a situation, the more chance you will have of getting a realistic, feasible *intelligent* solution.

You can also use external visual techniques, such as diagrams, mind maps, drawings and suchlike. Unlike lists, and left-to-right, top-to-bottom writing, these help to mirror the holistic way our right brain tends to work. When Einstein thought through a problem, he found it necessary to formulate his subject in as many different ways as possible, including using diagrams. He visualized solutions, and believed that words and numbers as such played a lesser role in his thinking process. Some people do this anyway. If it seems strange to you, do it for a few weeks and it will become a habit. *Train Your Brain* (published by Piatkus) covers the subject of creativity in some depth and give examples of graphical, diagrammatic and visual creativity techniques.

Visualization is strongly associated with:

- memory;
- goal setting;
- relaxation;
- focus;
- spelling ability;
- testing future scenarios;
- speed and 'photo-reading';
- creative problem solving;
- idea generation;
- skills improvement;
- sporting excellence;
- self-motivation;

and much more. Although visualization calls simply on the senses and imagination with which we are all blessed, it forms a big part of genius-level thinking. It is an example of 'sensory intelligence' and, most importantly, it can be readily improved with know-how and practice.

Make novel combinations

Look out for novel combinations. Mix and match ideas. In juxtaposition, things can take on a completely new significance. Combine and recombine ideas, images, and thoughts, no matter how unusual. Einstein didn't invent energy, mass and speed. He *combined* them in a way that gave us the equation $e=mc^2$ Leonardo da Vinci forced a relationship between the sound of a bell and a stone hitting water and established the fact that sound travels in waves. The intelligence feature is to connect the unconnected, and relate the unrelated.

We 'think' by putting things into compartments, to give them meaning, for future reference. That means that data is filed where it *originally* 'made sense' rather than in the best available state for some future purpose. Having said that, the sheer volume of data - a lifetime of sensory experience, and a mental landscape comprising a network of billions of neural connections - means that we typically have all the mental resources we need. We just need to access it and get it into a meaningful format. By recombining otherwise disparate bits of data, we increase exponentially the value of our recorded experience. Such a sophisticated search facility makes all the difference when confronting a new problem, or wanting special insight.

Fortunately this is an intuitive rather than cerebral, or cognitive process. That means that once you have mulled over a problem, set a goal, etc, your unconscious brain automatically goes to work on it. It happens *below the surface* of your conscious mind. Hence the occasional flash of inspiration, the 'eureka' moment, a sort of bubble of insight that rises into your conscious mind. Highly creative people make space and time for such creative moments.

Sleep on it

Sometimes things seem clearer after a good night's sleep. In fact, 'incubation', whether by day or night, is a vital part of normal brain operation. The clever work happens outside your conscious mind, perhaps while you are (consciously) thinking about other things, or during dream (REM) sleep. Thus, to recall something 'on the tip of your tongue' (which means on the threshold of your conscious mind), the trick is to *forget about it* (in practice, you need to think of something else). Then, sure enough, the word or memory will pop into your conscious mind after not too long. Insights of this sort range from simple, everyday sudden recollections, to mind-blowing revelations you would never have thought about with your conscious mind in a hundred years. They are a characteristic of super intelligence, but no less regular a function of the *normal brain*.

To tap this innate facility, you have to give your unconscious mind time and space to do its unique job. That means relaxing and giving your 'busy' mind a break. It means putting a matter out of your mind when you feel you are getting stuck, or becoming unduly worried or stressed. It means *trusting* your brain resources, even when there is time pressure, and a problem seems intractable.

Go for quantity

Produce as many ideas – of whatever quality – as you can. Generate as many *alternative* approaches as you can. Consider the least obvious as well as the most likely angles. Be willing to explore all options, even after finding a promising one. Carry on when other people stop. Quantity matters.

Geniuses think *productively*. Mozart produced more than 600 pieces of music. How many ever got to the stage or record companies? Bach wrote a cantata every week. Thomas Edison held 1,093 patents. Einstein didn't just write a learned paper on relativity theory; he published 248 others.

When confronted with a problem ask (in effect), 'How many different ways can I solve this? What is the *best* way? Can I turn this problem into an opportunity?' Go for multiple responses. Some may be impractical and on the face of it stupid. Some may be unconventional and some unique. But one good idea can change your life, so don't despair of unwieldy quantity in the creative process. Work on the assumption that there are countless ideas out there just waiting for someone to claim them – whoever is ready to.

Expect the unexpected

Any rational, planned process will tend to have built-in expectations. You don't get big surprises from a system that works consistently, logically and predictably, which is the way left-brain thinking tends to work. So it's a bit of a Catch 22. You need know-how, or a 'system', to produce ideas (or anything). You have to *do* something to make something happen. But, on the other hand, if you follow a system you will probably not get unexpected outcomes. Rather, you will get the sort of outcomes you might *expect* (from doing what you do, and from what the system was designed to do). Unconsciously, perhaps, your brain *runs the system* to see what might come out. And it stops there, either rationalizing 'impossible', 'will not work', etc or presenting the first feasible solution that occurs. Moreover, it tends not to run the system again (which it has probably run before when previously presented with such a question) if it thinks it knows the result. So it discounts, prejudges, assumes or whatever, sufficient to guarantee that existing mind patterns (all of them – sensible, true, right, familiar, etc) will not be disturbed. And that ensures a 'reproductive', me-too process that automatically filters out the novel, original or unexpected. You therefore not only stay in the mental rut, but the rut gets deeper and your prejudice stronger. The answer is to have a system that, as far as possible, guarantees an unexpected result by deliberately disturbing existing thought patterns. Expect – and only accept – the unexpected.

Change your perspective

Look at problems in many different ways, and find new perspectives that no one else has taken. Look for different meanings. See things as if through somebody else's eyes. You may have to abandon your initial approach, which will be based on past experience. The best problem-solvers not only solve problems, they identify new solutions of possibly greater significance and offering greater potential. Einstein's theory of relativity essentially described the interaction between different perspectives. One was sitting astride a beam of light. The *new perspective* provided the breakthrough. See the funny side. See the serious side. Think about the long term. Think as might a ten-year-old child, the Prince of Wales, a vicar, a life prisoner, your wisest friend. Change the context. What if this happened at work rather than at home, or vice versa? What if I faced this situation a year ago, a year from now? There are always new 'angles'. Seeing these is a feature of creativity. Don't go for a few degrees change in perspective. Turn things on their head, inside out, back to front.

Create ambivalence

Put up with instability, incongruence, and ambivalence. The physicist Niels Bohr had the ability to imagine light as both a particle and a wave, which led to his conception of the principle of complementarity (plus Nobel prizes and historical fame). Similar 'impossibility thinking' led to Einstein's breakthrough insight into the paradox of time and space. Living with ambivalence might take more effort for some people than others, depending on your disposition, but it can be developed by deliberate application. As with just about any trait, including the intelligence characteristic you have met, it can be learnt. Physicist and philosopher David Bohm believed geniuses were able to think different thoughts because they could tolerate ambivalence between opposites or two incompatible subjects. Be ready to think in opposites.

Ordinary left-brain thinking quickly rationalizes and eliminates possibilities that don't fit existing mindsets. It doesn't like even temporary uncertainty. In most situations that is fine, as in our day-to-day routine we follow a pattern of habitual behaviour that has served us well to date. We do what makes 'sense', without breaking any mental records, simply trusting our brain. However, by their very nature, completely novel situations (all too common when dealing with people, and rapidly changing technology) are too much for our existing, ingrained model of experience. They demand completely novel solutions.

The answer? *Don't do what you would normally do* to find a solution. Try something completely different. In particular, don't look for a sensible solution, or even a logical, or feasible one. We tend to think of sensible things first anyway, and have probably already tried that route. So, if 'black' would have been your normal approach, make it 'white'. If you would normally have gone faster, try going slower. If certain options seem impossible, imagine they were possible. Be contrary. Court ambivalence and uncertainty. Think in opposites.

Model your own creativity

Most of us get brainwaves from time to time and can recall times we might describe as creative or even 'brilliant'. These are mental resources worth utilizing to the full. If you consider yourself to have been something of a genius at some time or another (even for 15 minutes), try to relive your state of mind. Think back: What were the circumstances? How was I feeling? Who did I speak to? What triggered my state of 'flow'? What had I been thinking about before going off to sleep? How had I addressed my problem? Did I do anything on that day that I don't usually do - that might give a clue to my super creativity? What socks was I wearing? 'States' – what we *felt* at the time – form a vital part of memory, which is usually why we can recall certain childhood memories vividly. Positive, empowering memory states, including those associated with creative ideas and behaviour, are an important resource. To be able to draw upon 1,000 'intelligent moments' means that we can face just about any problem or challenge. Part of true intelligence is acquiring it, storing it, reusing it, and growing it in a purposeful way. It's within your control to improve and use as you will.

Think metaphorically

Aristotle considered metaphor a sign of genius. He believed that the individual who had the capacity to perceive resemblances between two separate areas of existence and link them together was a person of special gifts. Alexander Graham Bell compared the inner workings of the ear to a stout piece of membrane moving steel, and conceived the telephone. Metaphor and analogy are well-established characteristics of creative thinking.

An expert may have enormous reservoirs of knowledge but his or her ideas seem complex and unintelligible to others. He or she can't communicate them well. The secret of genius, rather than exaggerate the complexity and cloud the matter with mystique, is to make even the most complex subject simple enough for anyone to understand. The way that usually happens is by the use of metaphor, analogy and similes – by painting 'mind pictures'.

This extends to dreaming – including daydreaming – which has been the source of some of the most outstanding scientific breakthroughs. The right brain is especially associated with metaphor, stories and the nuance of meaning that we read 'between the lines'. Right-brain thinking is best done in a relaxed alpha, slow brainwave state. A workaholic, 'driven' type of person, even of very high intellectual intelligence and analytical powers, finds this very difficult. So not many such personalities reach the highest leadership positions – they burnout long before that level.

This is where self-knowledge and intrapersonal intelligence comes into their own. Reflection, goal setting and value setting as we covered in Chapter 3 may be the springboard for important changes in a person's life, and the door to another dimension of intelligence. A change of lifestyle may be needed. However, there is no shortage of books on relaxation techniques, and you may well have your own methods. Most of the suggestions in this chapter just need a simple act of will (you just *do it*), rather than special skill or a minimum entrance level of intelligence. The point about lifestyle changes is that we need to consciously *make time and space* for them. Our inarticulate, childlike, trusting, unconscious mind needs to do its job without the interference of our logical, 'know-all' left brain. It is a *non-trying* technique that eludes many so-called high achievers.

Take an interest

Some people seem interested in other people, their work, their family, their hobbies and interests and so on. Such a person seems to be always asking questions, willing to give things a try, willing to hear another point of view, willing to listen, ready to learn. Such people may not have a high IQ but, in the sense we have addressed in this book, they have a special kind of intelligence.

Learning from others doesn't cost you and can bring big benefits. New information may help to solve old problems beyond your own experience. New knowledge will give you new perspectives. You will see things from another point of view – through the eyes of somebody with different experience to you. Do you let the plumber do the job without watching, asking questions, and learning something? Do you miss the opportunity to learn about a subject you hadn't even heard of, that a friend or colleague seems keen to talk about? Do you let a word you don't know the meaning of slip by, again and again, without deliberately learning its meaning and using it yourself to enrich your language? Taking an interest, and grasping every learning opportunity, is a smart way to personal improvement, and a characteristic of mastery.

Create chances

Make space for chance. As golfer Gary Player used to say, 'The harder I practice, the luckier I get.' Learn from things that weren't intended to teach. In particular, learn from your mistakes. Make more if you need to, by attempting more. Expect happy circumstances and coincidences. They happen all the time and are no respecter of person, so you may as well enjoy your share. Don't expect bad luck. Why tempt misfortune? You get what you think about most and can always prove yourself right. Accidents – of any kind – provide useful lessons if we are willing to look on them in that way. Whenever we fail we simply get a different result from the one we expected. In the right frame of mind we can learn from what happened (or didn't happen). If you look for it, you can find benefit in *any* and *every* experience.

Benefiting from apparent chance happenings - creative accidents – is a feature of high intelligence, and can result in successes in widely different walks of life. Many scientific discoveries and inventions were put down to happy coincidence, or serendipity (this is covered in more detail in my book *Train Your Brain*).

You may ask yourself why you failed to do what you intended, which is a reasonable question. But the creative accident provokes different, smarter questions: 'What have I done?', 'What can I learn from this?' and 'What is interesting about what happened?'. Asking and answering such questions in a novel way is the essential creative act. The result may *appear* as luck, but this is in fact creative insight of the highest order.

Change

We tend to think more creatively when we get out of routine thinking and break habits. Thus, conditions of change and unfamiliar surroundings are good for new ideas. Often on holiday in a strange country we reflect on the direction of our lives, make important decisions and think of solutions to long-standing problems. This is a healthy mental process that we could benefit from much more. Sometimes on starting a new job, in a new organization and environment, we do our most productive work, which tails off after we have become 'part of the scenery' and run out of new ideas. A new town, a new home, a new school, however unnerving in the short term, can turn out to be landmarks of creative thinking and mental development. They can be mind enriching and foster true intelligence. Even brief 'changes of scenery' can feed your creative mind.

You can easily act on this mastery method. Think of 100 ways in which you can change. Here are some ideas to get started:

- move your furniture around frequently;
- change your route to work;
- take a holiday somewhere you would never have normally thought of going – or try a completely different kind of holiday;
- dress differently;
- change your hairstyle;
- take a different bus;
- sit somewhere different in the canteen;
- try different food;
- take up an unusual hobby;
- join a local special-interest group just for the fun of it;
- pretend (for one day for each) you are a bank clerk, a sculptor, a member of parliament or a prisoner in solitary confinement;
- watch different television programmes;
- read a different newspaper;
- buy a hobby magazine about something you know nothing about and read it from cover to cover, expecting useful, exciting new insights on your present life and circumstances;
- cut out television for a whole weekend.

When you open your mind to higher intelligence, change of any sort can be a sound investment. When you have important purposes (see the SMART goals criteria in Chapter 3) any experience can help towards their fulfilment, in ways you would never have imagined. When you have sorted out your values, any experience will be more meaningful, more significant, more enriching.

Change happens all around us, of course, sometimes at a dizzy pace, in such a way that we often don't seem to have any control over our future. The smart way is to make your own changes and start to create your own future.

Think laterally

Finally, a miscellany of factors associated with the best of human creativity and genius. There are no rules for becoming a genius. Most geniuses break the rules anyway. Nor can you turn lateral thinking on and off like analytical thinking. But there are plenty of ways to foster creative insights. Lateral thinking, paradoxically, requires some discipline, and there are common-sense principles you can apply. For instance:

Go for speed. This complements the 'quantity' principle of creativity you have met. Your intuitive mind works very fast indeed, and sometimes you have hardly got time to write ideas down. This applies especially to *visual* thinking. More importantly, by lingering too long on a specific idea (especially if it initially seems silly) you will give your slower but assertive left brain time to rationalize, criticize and argue it out of the running. Give your self a quota of ideas to get in say a 15-minute period.

Don't criticize your own or other people's ideas at the creative thinking stage. Criticism is an important, higher-brain function and an important aspect of intelligence. However, there is a time and place for criticism, and that is not at the very birth of ideas. Don't judge.

Don't discard. An untidy scientist did not discard a petri dish which, after a while became contaminated with a foul slimy mould. He was Alexander Fleming who, after pondering the strange growth, discovered penicillin. Don't go to bed without a pen and paper handy. A life-changing idea during the night might be lost in oblivion by the following day. Have a system of remembering ideas that come to you in the shower, when travelling, walking and so on. A single, quality insight can be of more value than many hours of hard thinking. Don't undervalue an idea because it came easily: it's much easier to be intelligent than dumb, so you may as well get used to the idea.

Don't conform. Be different in your approach. In a real sense, 'There is nothing new under the sun'. In other words, creative thinking is *recreative* thinking. You recreate your mental world to make more sense of the external world. Me-too thinking doesn't win Nobel prizes and nor will it outsmart business competitors. In fact it rarely pays the mortgage. We are all uniquely different, more so in our brain networks than fingerprints. Creative nonconformity reflects the way we are made. Don't think about other people's thoughts, at least when in brainstorming mood. Once you start putting your ideas through the 'what will he/she think' filter, they will soon dry up. Don't assume anyone is better qualified than you are to come up with an insight. Don't put your ideas through any filtering process. The best solutions often come from ideas that at first seemed the silliest.

Be ready to copy. There is no copyright on ideas. You can think what you like even if somebody else thought of it before. By the same token don't lose sleep if you find someone making a million on the idea you never got round to. Think about who might be able to help you. Geniuses can indulge in a little humility.

Don't develop ideas (too far). Once you start to think about implementation problems, downsides and obstacles you will need to engage your logical left brain and thus turn off your creative right brain. So ends your lateral thinking session. Making something work comes later. You may well require further lateral thinking once you have decided on the best course of action. Take one mental discovery step at a time. Standard genius does not extend to telling the future, so keep within your mental vision.

Don't get bogged down with detail. Walk away from a situation if you feel snowed under, or swamped with information. Have a break. Describe the problem or situation in one short sentence. If you can't, have another go in an hour or so.

Don't accept ideas as fully satisfactory. Assume there is a better, quicker, cheaper solution. Ready-made solutions can usually be made better. Perfect solutions can invariably be improved upon.

Ask lots of questions. At the same time allow for many of your questions to be stupid, or, at best, illogical. These usually turn out to be better questions, and, on average, good questions are better than good answers (really good questions almost answer themselves). Adopt questioning *behaviour* – tinker, find out how things work, play around, adapt, discover. Ask 'What if?' Asking questions is not a sign of what you don't know, but of what you believe you can know. There are no 'wrong' questions, but plenty that go unasked.

Don't try too hard. Don't hurt your brain for anything; it's all you have got and conscious, mental effort doesn't work anyway at this level of intelligence. Don't make an important decision that doesn't have to be made. By the time it does, you may have more information, the problem may have changed, or be overtaken by events. Or you may receive a 'eureka' insight before you have to make your decision. If at first you don't succeed, drop what you are doing and think about something quite different. Always be ready to walk away from a situation. Seen from further away, it may suggest a different meaning. The 'intelligent way' isn't always the macho, executive, 'do it now' way: it just works better, and takes less effort.

Believe there is a solution. There is always a way of achieving something. There is always a *better* way. True or untrue, these are valuable presuppositions to keep you in a creative, productive mode. It comes down to the intrapersonal competency of your willingness to 'believe' – especially in yourself. Self-belief underlies any sort of worthwhile achievement. Problems are problems because they don't lend themselves to a straightforward, logical solution based on conscious thinking. Intractable problems are intractable when we believe they are.

These simple rules apply when you want to get out of a thinking rut, and provoke your brain to come up with novel ideas. Each is of potentially very high value – that's the nature of creative, seminal thinking. Each, if carried out purposefully, will enhance some aspect of your intelligence. Together, and based on the intra- and interpersonal intelligences you have learnt about in this book, they can boost your true intelligence to a level that only you can limit.

Index

NB: numbers in italics indicate figures or diagrams